w4

£2-50
~~99p~~
Sale 10p

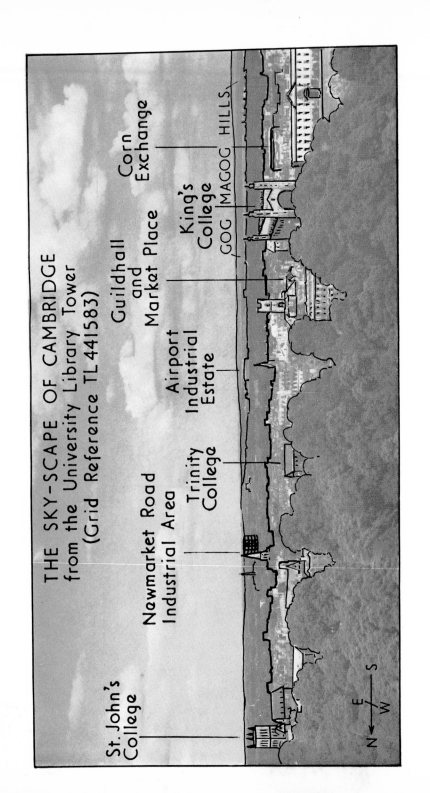

THE SKY-SCAPE OF CAMBRIDGE
from the University Library Tower
(Grid Reference TL 441583)

St. John's College

Newmarket Road Industrial Area

Trinity College

Airport Industrial Estate

Guildhall and Market Place

King's College

Corn Exchange

GOG MAGOG HILLS

A TOWN STUDY
COMPANION

First published 1969 by Hulton Educational Publications Ltd.,
55/59 Saffron Hill, London, E.C.1.
Printed in Great Britain by
John Gardner (Printers) Ltd., Liverpool 20

A TOWN STUDY COMPANION

G. B. G. Bull, M.A., Ph.D.

Head of the Department of Geography and Geology,
University of London Goldsmiths' College

HULTON EDUCATIONAL PUBLICATIONS LTD.

CONTENTS

THE OBJECT OF THE BOOK

Most of us now live in towns, and our numbers are increasing dramatically. In Great Britain, half the people live in the seven main "conurbations" of London, Birmingham, Liverpool, Manchester, Leeds, Bradford, Newcastle and Glasgow. If we include the medium and smaller towns, almost nine out of ten of us live in towns. To house our growing population, a planner has said, we shall need enough houses to fill a town of 50,000 people every seven weeks. It is clear that the great urban explosion is one of the decisive facts of our time.

The object of this book is to make us look more closely at towns, especially those in which we live. This book largely consists of questions designed to make us study the towns we live in or often pay visits to, with informed eyes, and to record in maps and in words what we have found out for ourselves. But, since our own town may lack examples of certain features common to most towns, we shall also find many questions on maps and drawings of other towns which possess particularly good examples of these features.

This is also a discussion book, whose purpose is to help us to argue about what is best and worst in towns as we find them, and to guide our thinking about the ways in which life in towns may be improved. Our study of towns as they are loses its purpose unless it leads on to planning for towns as they ought to be.

There is plenty of scope for differences of opinion about living in towns, and this should stimulate discussion among ourselves. To some of us, towns spell out work and amenities close at hand, shops and entertainments almost on our doorsteps and all the throb and gaiety of the urban mode of life. To others, towns mean traffic jams and din, queues at bus stops and shop counters, the deadly sameness of so many streets and shops, and the disease and squalor of the vanishing slums. Dr. Samuel Johnson held the view that, 'When a man is tired of London he is tired of life', but the poet Shelley wrote, 'Hell is a city very much like London.' Wordsworth wrote of the view from Westminster Bridge, 'Earth hath not anything to show more fair', but Rousseau held that 'Cities are the final pit of the human spirit.' Cowper, two hundred years ago, expressed the opinion that 'God made the country but Man made the town.' If he had lived a century later, he might have been moved to add, 'The Devil ran up the suburbs.'

1

FIELD WORK IN TOWNS: ITS AIMS

The aim of field studies in towns is to observe and to record what we find out. This is a valuable training in investigation, in recording neatly and accurately, and in thinking out the conclusions to be drawn from our observations. Remember that the scientist's method is to observe with care, and to set out clearly every piece of information which may be of later use. He eventually draws conclusions from the mass of recorded observations and seeks to use them for the betterment of mankind. Geographical field work, in town and country alike, is a means to the same end. The urban landscape is a laboratory – make full use of it!

FIELD SKETCHING FROM VIEWPOINTS

The first step in studying a town should be to go to a commanding viewpoint overlooking as much as possible of the whole built-up area, and to sit there for quite a long time taking in the view. Little by little, certain features will begin to stand out from the mass of chaotic detail, perhaps the high roof of a Town Hall which marks the centre of the town, some tall factory chimneys which mark the coming of industry to the town with the advent of railways, and an electric power station newly built on the fringes of the town to serve the swelling suburbs.

PANORAMIC SKETCHING FROM A PHOTOGRAPH

It may be helpful on the first visit to take a photograph from the lookout point and, when it has been printed, to draw on tracing paper laid over the picture a line which links up and passes along the upper edge of as many as possible of the points which seem to stand out. The result will be the outline of an urban silhouette. Simplify the outline as much as possible, so that it becomes a single, fairly smooth line above which the most prominent features project. Label these on the tracing, and stick the photograph and your annotated tracing in your record book. The black line drawn on the frontispiece shows the effect that can be obtained from this.

Did your annotated tracing from a photograph really satisfy you?

Did you not feel that the camera omitted many features because they were too far to the left or to the right of the view to appear in the picture?

Did you feel that certain things stood out in the photograph because they were big and close at hand, such as a gasholder or an advertisement hoarding, rather than outstanding features within the general picture of the town?

Did you not feel that some important things, such as a hill with one of the town's most popular parks upon it, failed to stand out because of their pale colour?

If you felt any of these things, you should try your hand at a field sketch from the point at which you took the photograph.

INSTRUCTIONS FOR DRAWING A SKY-SCAPE

1. Take with you to the viewpoint a very wide strip of paper, perhaps some four or five times as wide as it is high, a firm hard surface on which to rest it, such as a book or light drawing board, a well-sharpened pencil or two, and a clean rubber. Take also a map of the town, and a ruler.

2. Remember that what you need is not artistic ability to draw realistically what you see, but geographical ability to select and spotlight a few essentials in the view before you by means of a single line, or at most two or three lines.

3. The field sketch simplifies landscape by suppressing most of the detail in order to concentrate attention on the few meaningful features. Therefore, out with the hoarding or the gasworks if they detract from the purpose of the sketch, to draw attention to a few basic features of the town.

4. Do not draw the line a tiny piece at a time, but take a good long look, fix the shape of the line in your mind and then draw it as a whole. Then look at the view

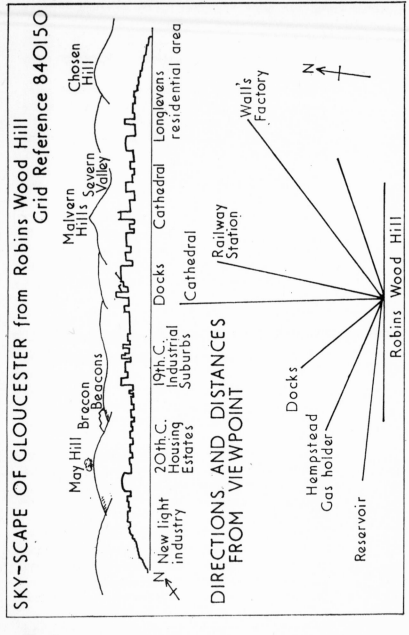

SKY-SCAPE OF GLOUCESTER from Robins Wood Hill
Grid Reference 840150

May Hill
Brecon Beacons
Malvern Hills
Severn Valley
Chosen Hill

New light industry
20th.C. Housing Estates
19th.C. Industrial Suburbs
Docks
Cathedral
Longlevens residential area

DIRECTIONS AND DISTANCES FROM VIEWPOINT

Cathedral
Railway Station
Wall's Factory
Docks
Hempstead Gas holder
Reservoir
Robins Wood Hill

N

Fig. 1

again, re-draw a bad piece or two, and then clean up the drawing with a rubber. Keep the sketch as neat and simple as you can.

5. Label the chief features, avoiding as far as possible too many or too long arrows. State below the drawing the name and grid reference of your viewpoint, and the direction in which you were looking (Fig. 1).

6. Now, having completed the sketch, unfold the map of the town and turn it so that it is stretched out in the same direction as the view. Identify on the map the features you have selected for emphasis on your field sketch, and attempt to find on the map a number of other points in the view, such as church spires, factory chimneys, and new housing estates which stand out fresh and clear because their buildings are so new.

7. Draw a series of lines radiating from a point, to represent the directions and distances (to scale) of prominent points in the town from the place where you have been sitting.

A SKY-SCAPE OF GLOUCESTER (fig. 1)

Here, in two lines, are the leading features of Gloucester, a city of 80,000 people, and of its setting among hills and vales. By looking at the sky-scape, one may almost trace the history of the town.

What is the oldest building shown, and how can you recognise it by its silhouette?

How can you recognise the area of docks and associated industries?

Can you recognise two gasholders?

Why do you think they have not been labelled, in spite of their size and prominence as skyline features?

In which direction has Gloucester grown most considerably, and in which direction has it grown least, according to the information given by the sky-scape?

Have buildings tended to become higher or lower through the ages?

Certain buildings are named in the diagram of directions and distances but are concealed behind other buildings in the sky-scape. What are these buildings?

What buildings appear in both?

Perhaps we should go to our viewpoint again, and try some-
thing else, a little more difficult but recording and revealing
more of the facts about the town.

FIELD SKETCH OF THE TOWNSCAPE OF NORWICH

Imagine that, seated upon St. James's Hill in the suburbs of
the city, we have sketched the silhouette of the central part of
the city. We now do this again, adding a few additional lines to
indicate the chief features in the middle distance and one or two
selected features from the foreground. Fig. 2 shows a silhouette
by means of the thick line in the background and also a fully-
developed field sketch, with the addition of selected details in the
foreground.

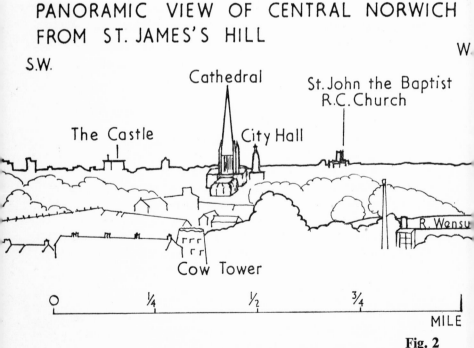

PANORAMIC VIEW OF CENTRAL NORWICH
FROM ST. JAMES'S HILL

S.W.　　　　　　　　　　　　　　　　　　　　　　W.

The Castle　　Cathedral　　City Hall　　St. John the Baptist R.C. Church

Cow Tower　　R. Wensu

0　　¼　　½　　¾　　MILE

Fig. 2

10

Bear in mind the following points:

1. Horizontal lines should be stressed to suggest flatness, where this is characteristic of certain areas, such as the mass of houses in the left foreground. Vertical lines should be stressed in areas with many changes of level, such as the area of factories set among trees in the right foreground.

2. Suppress insignificant detail, as in the houses in the immediate foreground where short horizontal strokes will convey the impression of the broken surface of a mass of houses.

3. Use thinner lines towards the background to convey the impression of receding distance. But use thick, firm and continuous lines to draw attention to any salient features such as the Castle, Cathedral and City Hall.

4. Incorporate in each part of the drawing some feature which conveys the impression of size. Thus in the foreground, the windows in the Bow Tower and the chimneys on the nearest house-roofs help to give this impression, while in the background the turrets on the roof of the City Hall and on St. John the Baptist's Church are helpful in showing their own sizes and in creating the impression of recession into the distance.

5. Remember to label the field sketch adequately, but at all costs to avoid congesting it.

FIELD SKETCHES OF THE TOWN'S PAST

The art of field sketching from a viewpoint gave pleasure, not only to present-day people, but also to artists of the 16th to 19th centuries, who often published panoramas either as illustrations to town-histories or as pictures to be hung on walls. The most attractive and revealing representations of the past of towns are to be found in these "long views" as they were called. The striking appearance of these panoramic views is often due, not so much to their accuracy, but to the subtle way in which they suppress minor detail and bring into prominence by slight exaggeration the most significant features in the prospect of the town. In short, a historical panorama by an artist such as Visscher or Hollar has for the geographer the merits of a field sketch made today.

It is very rewarding to discover one of the early artist's

panoramas of our town, to lay tracing paper over it and make a simplified tracing of the main features of the view as it was in the past, and to mount it in our record book. Side by side with this may be mounted our own field sketch made from exactly the same point. This gives us the opportunity to comment on the likenesses and differences between the town's past and present appearances.

PAST AND PRESENT IN GREENWICH AND THE ISLE OF DOGS

Fig. 3 shows in its upper part a simplified tracing from a view northwards from Greenwich Park over the River Thames and the Isle of Dogs drawn by Anthony van den Wyngaerde about 1558. A group of students was taken to the statue of General Wolfe which now stands at this viewpoint and given copies of this tracing. They were asked to draw over the tracing all features which were common to the landscape of 1558 and 1967. These were very few, merely the outline of the great U-shaped bend of the Thames enclosing the Isle of Dogs and th eridge of Epping Forest in the background. The students were then asked to add to their drawings the most important additions to the landscape since Elizabethan times, with the results shown in the lower part of Fig. 3.

St. Paul's Cathedral is the only building common to both views.

But has it been rebuilt?

What notable event in London's history, which took place in 1666, was responsible for the rebuilding?

Who was the architect of the new St. Paul's?

What are the likenesses and differences between the Royal Palace of Elizabethan times and the present-day Maritime Museum?

Dock cranes are easily identifiable on the lower sketch as slanting lines with a little hook at the top.

How many dock systems can you count?

Try to identify them with the aid of a fairly large-scale map of London.

Why do you think that these docks were constructed where we see them today?

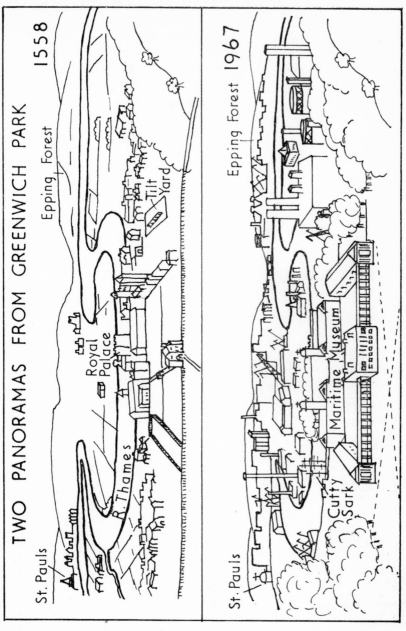

TWO PANORAMAS FROM GREENWICH PARK

1558

St. Pauls
Epping Forest
R.Thames
Royal Palace
Tilt Yard

1967

St. Pauls
Epping Forest
Cutty Sark
Maritime Museum

Fig. 3

13

A large gas works is identifiable by its gasholders, and the large building with four chimneys just to the left of them is an electricity generating station.

How can you account for their siting on the former Greenwich Marshes?

What do you know about the ship *Cutty Sark*, now in dry-dock near the National Maritime Museum?

What do you know about the Painted Hall in the Royal Naval College, which is situated just behind the point at which the word 'Maritime' appears on the sketch.?

The building in the background a little to the right of the very tall, thin chimney is a grain elevator, very similar to those built for storing grain in the Prairies of Canada, and filled by sucking the wheat up pipes.

How do you account for the presence of such a feature here?

THE FIELD SKETCH OF A BUILDING

In our walks through the town, our eye is often caught by a building which is of special interest, either because it stands out from its surroundings by reason of greater age or grandeur than the rest of the buildings, or because it is so typical of the district in which it stands that it seems worth selecting as a representative sample which sums up the character of the area as a whole. Any building of this kind is well worth a simple, well-labelled sketch, whether it be old and handsome or modern and utilitarian (Figs. 4 and 4a).

FIELD SKETCH OF AN INDUSTRIAL SCENE

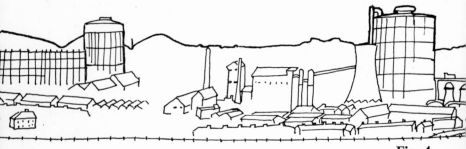

Fig. 4

14

A DERBYSHIRE TOWN HOUSE

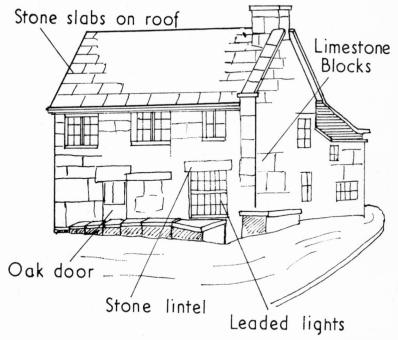

Stone slabs on roof

Limestone Blocks

Oak door

Stone lintel

Leaded lights

Fig. 4a

The labels should draw attention, in particular, to the materials used for the walls and the roof, and also to the age of the building where this is known. It will often be found that, if it is a very old building, it will be made of locally-available raw materials, such as local stone, or of timber framing with wattle and daub infilling. A building of great consequence, such as a mediaeval parish church, may be constructed of Portland Stone brought a long distance by sea, or some other classic building stone brought to the place at great expense. A building of the Railway Age or later will probably reveal the use of building materials brought from a long distance, such as slate from North

Wales, softwood timber imported into this country from the Baltic countries and Canada, concrete, non-local brick, steel and glass; sometimes with the wall covered by cement rendering, pebbledash or a cladding of weatherboard. External drain pipes, chimneys and the like may be made of metal and brought in from the hardware-manufacturing districts of the Midlands or from the potteries of Stoke-on-Trent or Swadlincote in Derbyshire. All such details should be noted in the labels accompanyin the sketch.

Labels should also draw attention to any details which reveal the function and purpose of the building (Figs. 5 and 6), especially if it has changed its use since it was built.

THE TOWN'S PAST IN ITS PRESENT

The starting point of our enquiry into a town's life and suitability for its purpose must always be what is visible at the present day – the town's "observables". But, as the enquiry proceeds, we shall be more and more drawn to study the town's past as an aid to understanding the present. So many features of the town's past live on, either as surviving buildings, as shapes or patterns in the layout of the town's streets and open spaces, or as memories and attitudes in the minds of the older people of the town who remember how the place used to look, that they strongly influence our present way of life. This is particularly true of those towns which have so many well-preserved old buildings that they possess a tourist industry which provides income for the shops, hotels and transport system.

FINDING AND USING EARLY MAPS AND PANORAMIC DRAWINGS

A visit to the Local History collection in the Reference Department of the larger Public Libraries will usually bring to light a printed book or two on local history and topography; with luck there may be found a multi-volume history of the whole county written in the eighteenth century, a shorter history of the town written in the nineteenth century, the Victoria County History compiled in the earlier years of the twentieth century,

OLD WEAVERS' COTTAGES, SEEL FOLD, UPPER MOSSLEY

Top storey used to run through both cottages.

Former doorway, for entry of wool, now blocked up

Fig. 5

WEAVER'S COTTAGE, MOSSLEY, LANCS.

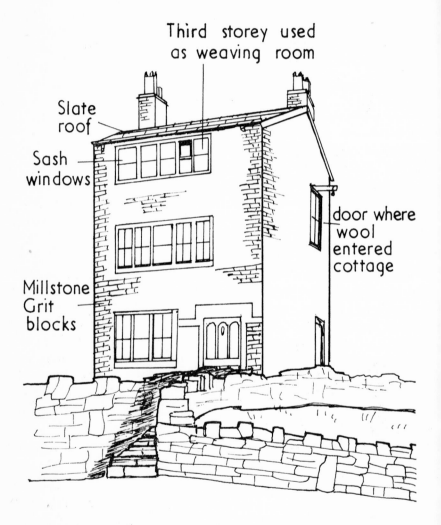

Third storey used as weaving room

Slate roof

Sash windows

Millstone Grit blocks

door where wool entered cottage

Fig. 6

and a well-illustrated account of the town's present and past published by the Town Council only a few years ago. There may also be a County Archaeological Society, Record Society or Field Club which publishes every year a number of short articles. A hunt through the index, or a courteous enquiry at the library's enquiry desk, will often aid in tracking down a useful reference or two.

Regrettably, local histories usually contain an excess of detail about churches and their monuments, and all too little about the homes and livelihoods of ordinary people in the past. It is therefore difficult to judge from books of this kind the facts about the past which have most influenced the present. Descriptions by travellers who visited the place in the eighteenth century, on the other hand, may be far more revealing than the rambling descriptions of churches and castles which fill so many local histories. For example, Daniel Defoe's crisp accounts of growing industrial towns in his *Tour through England and Wales* (1720) show the ways by which the workers of his time earned their bread.

It is local maps which prove their worth as essential background to geographical field study. Local history books may illustrate or refer to old maps or panoramic drawings made since the beginnings of these arts in the sixteenth century, but many more remain to be discovered. To ascertain what printed maps are available, the most useful handlists are *The Large Scale County Maps of the British Isles, 1596–1850*, by Elizabeth M. Rodger, published in 1960 by the Bodleian Library, Oxford, which can be bought quite cheaply, and Thomas Chubb's *The Printed Maps in the Atlases of Great Britain and Ireland*, published in 1927 and found in many good reference libraries. In addition, writers on map-making such as Sir Herbert Fordham, Thomas Chubb, Edward Lynam and R. A. Skelton have published books which give references to old maps and how they may be used as a tool for elucidating the present.

Many city libraries and county record offices now possess excellent collections of local maps and panoramas: both printed maps and the manuscript plans prepared to satisfy the requirements of Acts of Parliament. Three types of these deserve full description.

ENCLOSURE AWARDS

From about 1760 onwards, the normal method of enclosing commons or open fields was by private Act of Parliament. The Act authorized the appointment of commissioners to survey the lands to be enclosed. A large-scale plan of the lands was prepared, to assist the commissioners to draw up an award allocating the land to individuals. These awards, with their plans, record the boundaries of the fields and the courses and widths of the roads and trackways as laid out afresh by the enclosure commissioners. Occasionally this is accompanied by a map showing the pre-enclosure picture of open-field farming, with much land remaining as commons.

The value of enclosure maps is that they show the extent to which the old field boundaries and field trackways have helped to shape the pattern of the layout of Victorian and later streets and highways. Clearly, a Victorian estate builder would tend to buy a farmer's field and fill it with houses, thus preserving the old hedge-lines and access tracks, and even retaining the old name of the field, or the name of a politician or local hero of the time in some of the street-names of the estate.

This is clearly shown to be true of parts of Nottingham, in Fig. 41.

TITHE MAPS

Tithe maps, produced for the majority of places as a result of an Act passed in 1836 to convert into money rents the payments formerly made by landholders in kind to the Church authorities, give much information about field boundaries, the position of industries, crafts, workshops, inns and shops, and land use. A large scale plan showed each individual titheable plot (omitting those which were exempted), numbered to correspond with entries in an Apportionment or register which stated the owner and occupier of the land, the area and the current land use.

Copies of Enclosure and Tithe Awards were deposited in each parish, usually in the parish chest kept in church or vicarage, with duplicates in the office of an official known as the Clerk of the Peace. These have often been collected into the County or City Record Office, which may be able to have photographs made of these very large maps, as the originals are often fragile and difficult to study because of their very large size.

DEPOSITED PLANS OF PROJECTED CANALS AND RAILWAYS

When a railway or canal was projected, even if it was never actually built, a map of the strip of land affected was by law given to each landowner, with another copy for the Clerk of the Peace and a third for the Railway or Canal Company. Many maps and plans of this kind are to be found in County Record Offices and in the records of the British Transport Commission. References to books on canal or railway history may disclose whether such maps or plans are likely to be found.

PREPARATIONS FOR FIELD MAPPING IN A TOWN

The most fundamental kinds of urban fieldwork consist of taking into the streets a large-scale Ordnance Survey Map in order to add to it information as this is observed. These maps, obtainable from Edward Stanford Ltd., 12–14, Long Acre, London, W.C.2., are available on various scales. Probably the most useful for the field mapping of a town centre is that on the scale of 25 inches to a mile, with a representative fraction of 1/2,500, but, if the area is very congested with small buildings, it may be preferable to use the plan on the scale of 50 inches to one mile, or 1/1,250 if available. For a more general view of the whole or greater part of a town, the map on a scale of 6 inches to one mile or 1/10,500 is available, but individual buildings are almost too small to identify at this scale. An even more general view, in which the detail of individual buildings is entirely lost, is the map on the scale of $2\frac{1}{2}$ inches to a mile, or 1/25,000. This map has the advantage that it has contours at 25 foot intervals: the others may have no contours at all, or at infrequent intervals.

Since Ordnance Survey maps are costly, and large, it is an advantage to prepare outline base maps by tracing, and to carry these into the streets for use in recording your observations. Always make a second copy so that you can make a fair copy, preferably in colour, of the information which you have inserted by the use of letters, numbers or symbols on your field map. While it saves time if your field maps are neat enough to be inserted into your field book, it usually becomes necessary for fair copies to be made before inserting them.

THE TOWN'S PAST IN ITS PRESENT

2

It is important, when studying the oldest parts of a town, to find out the extent to which ancient patterns of town planning have influenced the present arrangement of streets and buildings, despite centuries of rebuilding and replacement which may have in fact done away with every really ancient building. By knowing a little about the ways in which towns have been planned in past ages, we may be in a better position to appreciate the impress of the past upon the present structure of our town centres.

Towns, it has often been said, are as old as civilization. Why is this? It is because there is a common geographical basis for both the rise of civilization and for the gathering of men to live in groups which are too large to feed themselves from the ground on which they dwell. Urban communities can be supported only when material conditions are such that there is a surplus of food over and above the consuming needs of the food-growers, and when the means of transport are also available to concentrate the food surplus at particular spots. In these spots, and supported by this food, are concentrated people who have certain skills for which the farmers are willing to pay.

THE IRON AGE HILL TOWN

Garn Boduan in Caernarvonshire (Fig. 7) is an example of the earliest type of town to evolve in Britain, not long before the Roman occupation. It is situated on a hill-top, protected in some parts by the steep crags represented by wedge-shaped marks, and enclosed in others by a massive bank of earth and stones bounded by a deep ditch. Iron Age peoples erected the defences and lived within them in pits roofed over with cones of poles covered with twigs, heather or ferns from the moorlands in the vicinity. These are shown by means of small circles.

Study the sketch map and try to answer the following questions about it.

GARN BODUAN
Caernarvonshire

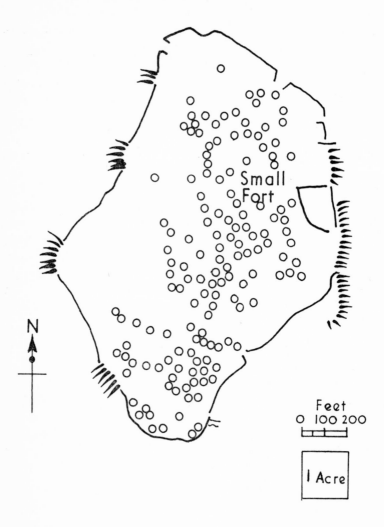

Small Fort

N

Feet
0 100 200

1 Acre

Fig. 7

What is the evidence that defensive needs were partly responsible for the assembly of a considerable number of people in Garn Boduan?

How many people lived in it at one time? (Start by counting the pits, but halve the number on the grounds that some of the pits were used for storage and that not all those used for houses were in use at any one time. Assume that each inhabited pit was the home of a family of four people.)

What is the approximate area in acres of the entire settlement?

What was the density of population? (Divide the number of people by the number of acres.)

How does this compare with the population density in a modern town?

How far apart are the houses on the average?

Is there any evidence that defence and housing were not the only purposes of the enclosure?

What use might have been made by the community of the vacant space?

Is it likely to have been cultivated? Would cattle have been kept there in times of war?

Evidence of smelting iron with charcoal was found by the excavators of the site.

Is it likely that an embankment of this length and size could have been made before the Iron Age?

What is the length of the embankment?

Why is it not continuous all round the site?

How many entrances has it?

Are they evenly spaced?

From what directions did those who required the craftsmen's services tend to come?

What did they bring to fill the needs of the people on this bleak hill-top?

Many similar embanked enclosures are known, usually on hill-tops but not invariably sited on high ground.

Can you find out some facts about Maiden Castle, just outside the present town of Dorchester in Dorset, or St. Catherine's Hill, outside Winchester, Hampshire? These have survived intact because they were abandoned by their populations after a century or two; there were others on lower ground which have been occupied in whole or part ever since. Of course, the Iron Age banks and ditches have been levelled, so that the only traces of their presence are Iron Age relics found by excavators in digging across their remains, or in the alignment of roads which once served the Iron Age town.

Are there any examples in the town you are studying? Look at the sketch map of Winchester (Fig. 8), and particularly its western end. Note the section of the town now known as Oram's Arbour, which was partly enclosed by a bank and ditch (the City Ditch) until they became a nuisance and were levelled about 1700.

WINCHESTER'S STREET PATTERN

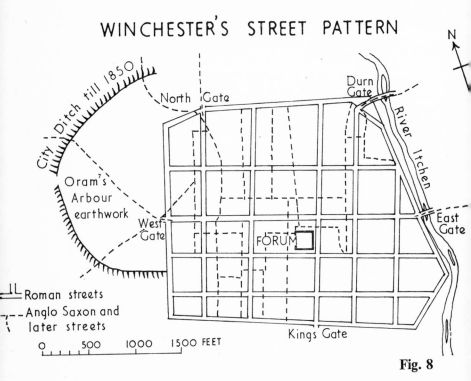

Fig. 8

Do you think that the name 'Oram's Arbour' has any meaning to recent generations in Winchester or is it the sort of name which has become so altered over many centuries that its origin has been forgotten?

If Oram's Arbour had once been part of an oval Iron Age town, how many feet was it in length and breadth?

How does this size compare with that of your own town?

Was it smaller or larger than Garn Boduan (Fig. 7)?
Excavation of the filler in the ditch of Oram's Arbour in 1965 revealed Iron Age pottery, Roman coarseware made in the New Forest of Hampshire, and a third-century coin.

What do these finds show?

The ditch was originally 13 feet deep and about 25 feet wide.

How many cubic feet of earth would have to be extracted to make a 10 foot section of ditch?

If a cubic foot of earth weighs about 50 lbs., how many tons of earth needed to be shifted per 10 feet of ditch?

ROMAN TOWNS

When the Romans conquered Britain in 43 A.D., they set about imposing their civilization in the way they knew best – by providing it with towns and joining them up by roads. Every town laid out by the Romans was arranged on a chess board or grid iron plan of intersecting streets, and was usually protected by a massive square stone wall with a gate in the middle of each side. Most of these towns came into existence as fortified places; the Roman word 'castrum' or 'chester' means 'a military encampment'. Almost all the towns whose names end in this way, such as Winchester, Chichester, Dorchester and Manchester, as well as those whose name endings have been modified, such as Lancaster, Worcester and Gloucester, began their existence as Roman fortified places.

The core of the city was the Forum, a group of buildings which comprised the town hall, the court of justice, a shopping centre and spacious meeting place for the people of the town and its surrounding countryside. Roman ideas in town planning were fundamental to the later development of the English town.

Is there any evidence of Roman influence in the lay-out of the streets of your town?

Study the town-plan of Winchester (Fig. 8).

What are its dimensions from north to south and from east to west? Assuming it to be rectangular, what is its area?

Assuming that the population of Roman Winchester

numbered 5000, what was the density of population per acre?

How does this compare with the density in Garn Boduan (Fig. 7)?

Why was the River Itchen relatively easy to cross near Durn Gate and East Gate?

Was there a marked degree of continuity between the streets of Roman Winchester and those of Anglo-Saxon and later times? (We may assume that the town became abandoned soon after the Romans departed, and the buildings collapsed and blocked the main streets, necessitating a fresh layout of streets when the town was re-occupied by Anglo-Saxons.)

The Anglo-Saxon Cathedral occupies the approximate site of the Forum.

Why was this?

THE ANGLO-SAXON AND NORMAN BOROUGH

The Anglo-Saxon invaders who arrived in the fifth to seventh centuries were tillers of the soil, not interested in repairing the roads or maintaining the towns which fell into partial disuse. The Anglo-Saxons at first regarded towns as 'the defences of slavery and the graves of freedom . . . the work of giants seen from afar'. The scene was changed when the Vikings from Scandinavia overran the east and north of the country in the ninth century, and turned to town life in the area which they conquered, the Danelaw. The commercial life of York, their headquarters from 876, was revived by Viking enterprise, the Roman walls of Chester were rebuilt by a Viking chief, and the East Midlands came under the jurisdiction of the five newly-created Scandinavian boroughs of Nottingham, Derby, Leicester, Stamford and Lincoln. The Anglo-Saxons, under their kings Alfred the Great and Edward the Elder, not to be outdone, also created boroughs similar to those of the Scandinavian invaders, at places such as Northampton, Huntingdon, Bedford and Tamworth, and despite many setbacks, reconquered all the territory which the Scandinavians had acquired. In 1066, the Normans in their turn came to Britain as conquering invaders, and also built new boroughs and enlarged old ones.

The Anglo-Saxon, Scandinavian and Norman borough had varied functions. It was foremost a defended place or strong point surrounded by an earthen bank of oval or square shape, or by the patched-up wall of an older Roman town. In each new borough, the King settled a permanent garrison with ample reserves, sustained by landowners on whom was laid the obligation of defending the borough in time of need. In return for this, the borough and its burgesses were protected by the King's special peace. The borough was also a trading centre, with a market place and often a mint for coins. When King Edward the Elder ordained that all buying and selling should take place in a market town in the presence of a town-reeve, he ensured the concentration of trading in the growing boroughs.

The borough was also an administrative centre. Indeed, many of our modern counties came into being as the territories allocated by the King to the support of the defences and trading facilities of a borough, e.g. Nottinghamshire was the support for the county town of Nottingham, as its name shows.

Nottingham, as shown in Figs. 9 and 10, was a Scandinavian borough enlarged by the Normans after 1066.

CENTRAL NOTTINGHAM

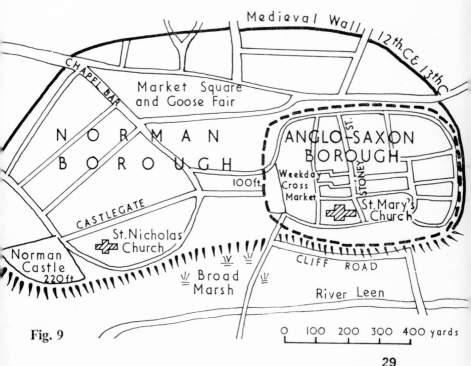

Fig. 9

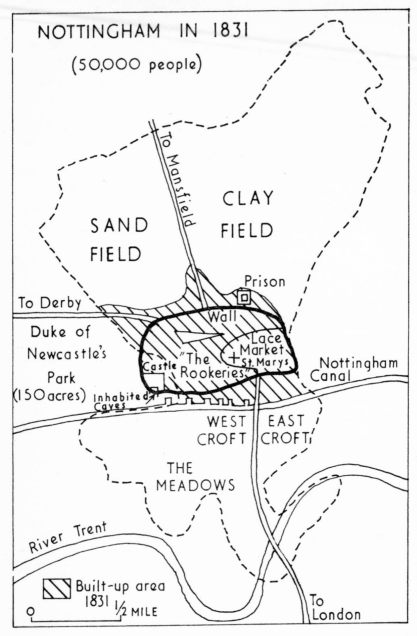

Fig. 10

THE MEDIAEVAL CASTLE-TOWN

The Normans concentrated the defence of the country in castles, which began to be built all over the country. In many places where a castle was built in a strategically important position, especially in regions liable to attack such as the Scottish and Welsh borders, a new town began to cluster round it, seeking its protection and supplying its daily needs. Such towns as Arundel, Alnwick, Devizes, Barnard Castle, Launceston, Ludlow, Newcastle upon Tyne, Pontefract and Richmond (Yorkshire) all grew up in the shelter of great Norman castles, and many of them were provided with walls.

> If there was a Norman castle in your town, make a plan of it. See if it is an early Norman castle mentioned in Domesday Book.
> If so, find out how much Domesday Book has to say about the town itself.

Conway (Fig. 11) is a little exceptional in that the castle and walled town were both planned and built at one time, by King Edward I as part of his plan for the conquest of Wales.

The town wall has many bastions, i.e. semi-circular bulges.

> What is the function of these?
> In what ways does Conway resemble and differ from a Roman town?
> What is the central building in the town of Conway?

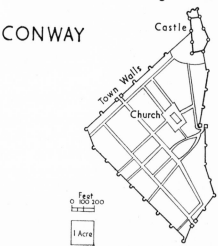

CONWAY

Castle

Town Walls

Church

Feet
0 100 200

1 Acre

Fig. 11

MARKETS AND FAIRS

Most boroughs came into being through the action of the King or some great noble or bishop in selecting a strong point, primarily as a centre of defence, in late Anglo-Saxon or early Norman times. In the more peaceful days, the twelfth and thirteenth centuries, town burgesses began to increase their freedom to control markets and trade by purchasing charters, or documents setting out the town's right to the status of borough, free to conduct its own affairs in return for an annual payment to the King. The wording of the charter often included the right to hold a weekly market and an annual fair. The market was the most important weekly event in the life of a mediaeval town, and the essential nucleus of the town became the market square. This was the place where agricultural produce from the surrounding countryside could be sold, and where the town craftsmen could display their wares. Stalls and booths, at first temporary and later permanent, began to be erected in the centre of the market place, and outlying parts of the market were set aside for the sale of livestock. Later, many towns acquired a market hall, or town hall, with a meeting hall for the transaction of business on the upper floor and open arches at ground level where goods might be displayed out of the rain.

The market was concerned with supplying local needs; fairs had a wider significance because they attracted traders from other parts of England and even from the Continent. Here one might buy the specialised products of certain parts of England, such as Sussex iron, Worcestershire salt, Derbyshire lead or Cornish tin, or spectacle lenses ground at Augsburg in Germany, beaten copperware from Dinant in modern Belgium or cutlery from Solingen in Germany.

As towns began to assume self-government, they had to work out the best ways of controlling industry and trade. An elected council met in a moot hall or town hall, with a common seal to impress on documents as guarantees that they were genuine, a mayor to preside over the meetings, a mace to carry before him to symbolize his power to quell disturbances, and special robes for the aldermen and councillors to wear in order that all citizens might be able to recognize them and do them honour. The town council dealt with the problems of the whole town, but rarely had the specialized knowledge which is necessary to regulate a craft such as tailoring or silverwork.

CRAFT GUILDS

In the later part of the Middle Ages, especially after the Black Death which first occurred in 1348 and had reduced the population of Britain by a third, thus creating shortages of labour, guilds or societies of qualified workers in a single craft began to be formed. Towns with varied industries such as York or Newcastle-on-Tyne each had about sixty different guilds; Gloucester, which was a port rather than a craft town and which specialized in woollen cloth-making, had only eleven craft guilds.

The craft guilds often built their own guildhalls, particularly in the larger cities like London and York, elected their own officials who conducted tests to decide whether young craftsmen were sufficiently well-trained to be admitted to the guild, and also looked after their members who were too ill or old to work. Nearly every guild had a religious background, adopting the name of a patron saint, maintaining a chapel in the parish church with a chantry priest to pray for the souls of dead guildsmen, and performing open-air plays and pageants recalling the great deeds of the saint. Many guilds built almshouses, often known as hospitals, for aged members or their widows, and some of them built free schools, as at Worcester, Ludlow and Bristol. Unfortunately, the guilds came in time to use their power in ways which restricted trade, and therefore the citizens deemed them harmful and dissolved them. Many of today's towns, however, have visual reminders of the craft guilds of the later Middle Ages in the form of guild chapels and ancient almshouses.

TUDOR AND JACOBEAN TOWN HOUSES

In the Middle Ages, the craft guilds ensured that, although few craftsmen were really poor, few were so much richer than their fellows that they could afford to live in luxurious houses. By the sixteenth century, however, when the Tudor kings and queens ruled, the weakening of the craft guilds at a time when the cloth industry was booming, enabled a few cloth merchants and manufacturers to amass fortunes. These they spent in replacing their mean craftsmen's premises by substantial and comfortable dwellings, such as that shown in Fig. 12 (top left).

Study this, and answer the following questions.

The building has a timber frame, often painted black, with an infilling of whitewashed plaster over a light framework of interwoven split sticks (wattle and daub).

Assuming the door is 6 feet high, how many feet of timber were required to make the exposed beams?

Why are such houses often called 'magpie' or 'black-and-white' houses?

Why are they more numerous in the well-wooded west, south-east and midlands of England than in East Anglia or Lincolnshire?

The work rooms upstairs are more roomy than the living rooms and shop premises downstairs.

How is this brought about?

There are more and larger windows upstairs than downstairs.

Why is this?

How does an Elizabethan shopfront differ from a modern one?

Are there any Tudor town houses or inns in your town?

If so, draw or photograph them and find out all you can about what purpose they were built for and how they are used today.

QUEEN ANNE TOWN HOUSES

Following the turmoil of the Civil War of Charles I's reign and the decay of trade which lasted for most of the Stuart period, England settled down to an age when town houses were not built with pomp and ostentation but with comfort and elegance. The early eighteenth century was a time when many towns became centres of culture and style, and built for themselves fine assembly rooms, coffee houses, theatres and fashionable shops. A craze for 'taking the water' at spas with mineral springs was born, and places like Bath, Droitwich, Tunbridge Wells, Cheltenham and Harrogate shared in a wave of building which had elegance and individuality as its keynote.

GUILDHALL,
THAXTED, Essex
15th. C.

TOWN WALLING-
HALL FORD,
Berks.
1670

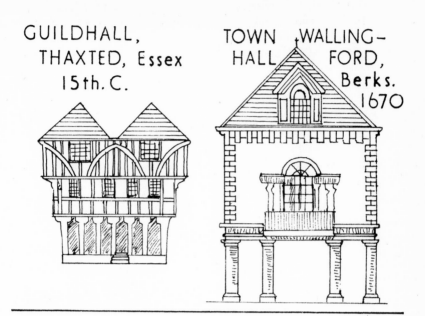

GUILDHALL,
BATH, Somerset   1776

Fig. 12

Fig. 13 shows part of streets in two of these towns.

The houses, although very similar in architectural style, differ very greatly in width and height.

What are the features common to almost all the houses?

How do they differ?

Do you agree with those who say that irregularity of width and height adds beauty to a street?

Should streets be planned as wholes or should they be allowed to grow by addition?

Wrought ironwork is a feature of Queen Anne houses. How does it appear in the street shown?

A common architectural feature of this period is the pilaster, i.e. a thin strip of stonework or painted plaster which from a distance looks like a solid pillar.

Do you find pilasters beautiful adornments to buildings, or do you think they are useless shams which serve no purpose?

Where were the servants' rooms in these Queen Anne houses?

The roofs which are very steep pitched can be seen clearly from below.

Do you think that house roofs should be clearly visible or should they be low pitched and hidden behind parapets?

What Queen Anne buildings are still to be seen in your town?

Draw or photograph them, and find out about their history and present day uses.

Some famous architects building in Queen Anne style were Sir Christopher Wren (1632–1723), Sir John Vanbrugh (1664–1726), Nicholas Hawksmoor (1661–1736), Thomas Archer (1668–1743) and James Gibbs (1683–1754).

Are there any examples of the work of these architects, or of their pupils, in your town?

REGENCY STYLE

The wealth gained from a growing Empire in Canada and India made possible an 'Age of Elegance' towards the close of the eighteenth century. For many years, King George III was too ill to rule and the reins of power were in the hands of the Prince

A REGENCY TERRACE IN A SMALL TOWN
c. 1820

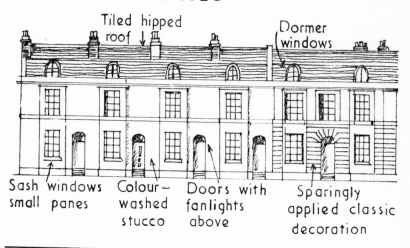

Tiled hipped roof ↓

Dormer windows

Sash windows small panes

Colour-washed stucco

Doors with fanlights above

Sparingly applied classic decoration

REGENCY TERRACE IN A LARGE TOWN

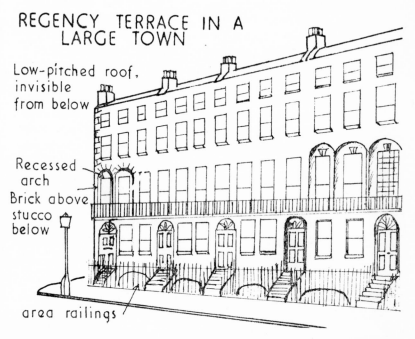

Low-pitched roof, invisible from below

Recessed arch
Brick above stucco below

area railings

Fig. 13

Regent, George, Prince of Wales. Hence the distinctive style of architecture which marks the closing years of the eighteenth century is called 'Regency'.

It was an age of town-planning; when terraces of houses were planned with fairly uniform height and width to achieve a well-composed facade. The planned terraces were arranged in carefully designed sequences of squares, crescents and circuses linked by straight streets of simple design.

The classical buildings of Greece and Rome provided much inspiration for Regency architects (Fig. 15). Pillars supporting porticoes for main doors, tastefully moulded shell-mouldings above lesser doors, and windowheads in classical designs, were features of the richest town houses, but our illustrations show middle-class houses of simpler but equally tasteful design.

How do the terrace houses in a small town differ from those of a large town (Fig. 13)?

How do the roofs of Regency houses differ from those of Queen Anne houses?

Decoration of Regency houses was sparing, but effective.

Of what does it consist?

The 'large town' terrace, built by Nicholas Barbon, a great London builder, consists of uniform houses, with a 20 foot frontage, two rooms in depth. The kitchen and housekeeper's room were in the basement, the eating-room and a bedchamber on the ground floor, the parlour and another bedchamber on the first floor, three more bedchambers on the second floor and garrets for the servants in the roof.

Do you think that these very narrow and tall houses are conveniently arranged, particularly today when resident servants are not easily available?

What Regency houses are to be seen in your town?

What sort of people lived in them when they were built and how are they used today?

THE LEGACY OF THE INDUSTRIAL REVOLUTION TO TOWNSCAPES

The Industrial Revolution was a great economic upheaval which transformed Britain from an agricultural nation into one of the world's leading centres of industry. This transformation was made possible by a crop of inventions of machines between the years 1750 and 1850. Hargreaves' Spinning Jenny in 1767 and James Watt's improved steam engine in 1769 were among the inventions which drew countrywide workers in tens of thousands to migrate to those towns where work with machines was available, making mass-produced goods which formerly had been hand-made by craftsmen. Industry grew most rapidly in the narrow valleys of the Pennines and of South Wales where water power could be harnessed to work machines, and later in the nearby coalfields of Midland and Northern England, as steam-power took over the function of water-power.

The expansion of coalmining and iron-smelting in the Black Country of the Midlands, the growth of the woollen industry of Yorkshire and the cotton industry of Lancashire led to an upsurge of town life which was to crowd more and more people into towns dominated by industry.

THE REVIVAL OF THE ARCHITECTURAL STYLE OF ANTIQUITY

The architecture of the Industrial Revolution period ran to extremes. At one end of the scale, a certain number of very grand and ostentatious buildings were erected for display; at the other, a mass of humble and undistinguished terraced houses were built as dwellings for the industrial workers.

The grander buildings, such as Town Halls and residences for richer folk such as factory owners, tended to be built in architectural styles which sought to adapt features copied from the buildings of Greek, Roman, Egyptian and Mediaeval periods to the needs of the time. Since long iron girders were available to the nineteenth century builders whereas the classical and mediaeval architects were limited to masonry, it was natural that the new buildings were on a scale unknown to the ancients, and called on the past mainly for decorative adornments.

Fig. 14 shows some of the Egyptian decorative features which were adapted by Isambard Kingdom Brunel to the decoration of the Clifton Suspension Bridge (1836–64). Fig. 15 shows similar ideas adapted to the adornment of the façade of the so-called

39

Egyptian Institute at Plymouth in 1823. The same view shows extensive use of columns copied from Greek and Roman buildings of the various periods shown in the bottom half.

Congleton Town Hall (Fig. 16) shows a combination of features selected from mediaeval or Gothic buildings, particularly churches. Some Gothic features, too, are evident in the houses of the wealthy suburban dwellers, such as the Red House built by the popular artist William Morris at Bexleyheath in 1859, and a house built for an Oxford Professor in Banbury Road, Oxford, in 1877 (Fig. 17).

> Draw and describe any buildings in your own town which derive from Egyptian, Greek, Roman or Gothic originals, or which incorporate architectural features of these periods.
>
> What Egyptian motifs are evident in the Clifton Suspension Bridge and the Egyptian Institute?
>
> What features of Gothic architecture are common both to the Town Hall and the private residences?

VICTORIAN TERRACE HOUSING

In the early days of the Industrial Revolution when the workers spun and wove cloth or hammered metal in their own homes, they erected austere but well-proportioned industrial cottages of local stone with workrooms in their upper stories. Later, when they worked in factories, they lived in terraces of uniform two-storeyed dwellings built of brick and slate brought by the new railways and canals. The less fortunate suffered deplorable living conditions in crowded tenements and back-to-back houses in narrow courts; the remainder endured the deadly monotony of endless views of ribbed slate rooftops, bristling with smoking domestic chimneys, broken at intervals by higher, more massive, public buildings such as churches, schools and hospitals, and the multi-storeyed factories and gasworks whose chimneys form the chief features of these monotonous tracts of townscape. This endless repetition reflects the way in which local by-laws demanded certain standards in height of house, width of street, height of rooms and so on; this conformity led to machine-like repetition of standardized housing. Streets, too,

40

EGYPTIAN REVIVAL STYLES

Clifton Suspension Bridge, designed by Isambard Kingdom Brunel, 1836-64

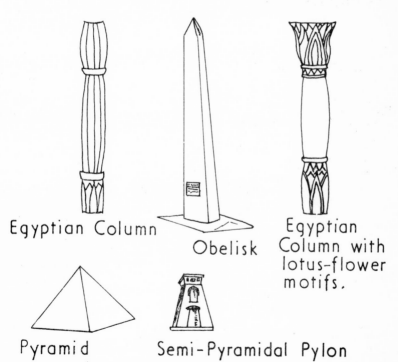

Egyptian Column

Obelisk

Egyptian Column with lotus-flower motifs.

Pyramid

Semi-Pyramidal Pylon

Fig. 14

MIXED ARCHITECTURAL STYLES
Devonport, Plymouth, Devon, 1823

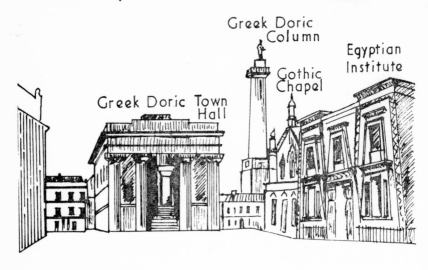

Greek Doric Column

Egyptian Institute

Gothic Chapel

Greek Doric Town Hall

GREEK AND ROMAN REVIVAL STYLES

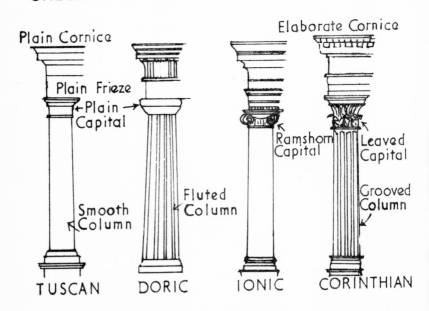

Plain Cornice

Elaborate Cornice

Plain Frieze

←Plain → Capital

Ramshorn Capital

Leaved Capital

Grooved Column

Fluted Column

Smooth Column

TUSCAN   DORIC   IONIC   CORINTHIAN

Fig. 15

GOTHIC REVIVAL STYLE
Congleton Town Hall, Cheshire - 1864

Rose Window

Ogive Window

Lancet Window

Machicolated Wall

Gable Window

Buttress

Fig. 16

THE RED HOUSE, BEXLEYHEATH, KENT 1859

PROFESSOR'S HOUSE, NORTH OXFORD 1877

Fig. 17

became of standard size, with no difference between those taking wheeled traffic and those taking pedestrians. There was no sorting out of functions; warehouses, streets of houses, factories, parks and cemeteries stood side by side (Fig. 41). This arrangement at least had the merit of allowing the worker to live close to his place of employment, and his children to have a short journey to school, but the regimented uniformity was a burden to the human spirit.

THE POST-VICTORIAN SUBURB

During the Industrial Revolution, railways brought people into towns to live near their work. Public transport since about 1880 has been taking people away from town centres to create modern suburbs. Tramcars and suburban railway lines began the change; it was continued by buses and trolley buses and now increasingly by private cars. This ease of movement, together with a desire for a private garden, for tree-lined roads and a break from the dull uniformity of terrace living, led to the building of detached villas for the wealthy, semi-detached villas for those who wished to own their own houses, and council estates for those who preferred to rent their dwellings. Suburbia and council estates are easily recognized on a map because the houses stud the landscape rather than make continuous ribs across it, and because the pattern of streets contains many curves instead of being made up entirely of straight lines. The emphasis on the housing needs of the single family is very apparent. So too is a craving for individuality in design; it is possible to find streets of semi-detached houses in which every pair of houses differs from all its neighbours, often by introducing all sorts of architectural devices to recall the past, as in 'Stockbroker's Tudor' and 'Bypass Variegated'.

STOCKBROKER'S TUDOR (fig. 18)

The Great War of 1914–18 was a time of disillusionment, which caused many wealthy folk to try to turn back the clock of history and to recreate in the houses which they erected 'the spacious days of Great Elizabeth', the last Tudor queen. These were 'olde-worlde' houses in appearance, but contained twentieth century comforts. Many of the apparent timber beams were only strips of wood stuck over plastered brickwork, the rustic-looking shed beside the house was in fact a garage for one or two cars, the barley-sugar-twisted chimneys were often shams, since the fires in the house were electric or gas, even though logs of gauze containing light-bulbs appeared to blaze in cast-iron grates. Above the front door, what appeared to be a horn lantern contained an electric light-bulb. The leaded window-frames and panes containing small discs of bottle-glass were scientifically mass-produced in a factory. The old oak beams which supported the ceiling in the lounge were in fact hollow frames to conceal the steel girders which bore the weight of walls and roof.

What is your opinion of 'Stockbroker's Tudor'?

Is it wise to spend money in recreating an 'olde-worlde' atmosphere?

Such a house needs to be furnished with antiques or sham antiques, such as four-poster beds, straight-backed settees without cushions, and old oak chests.

Is such furniture comfortable and does it look good?

'WIMBLEDON TRANSITIONAL' (fig. 18)

In the 1920's and 1930's many of the features of the 'Stock-broker's Tudor' style were copied, in cheaper form, by the much wider public who were having houses erected in the newer suburbs. From the houses of the wealthy were imitated the mock beams, but these merely consisted of thin painted slats of wood ornamenting the large gable which was the principal feature of the façade. Another sham antique feature was the use of pebble-dash to fill the spaces between the sham timbers; tiny pebbles were pressed into wet concrete to produce a rough surface. Weather-boarding was also used to give a sham antique finish to surfaces; thin narrow planks to hide the brickwork of which the walls were constructed.

Other features were novel, notably the use of white-painted wooden porches, verandahs and conservatories. There was a small garden between the front-door and the road, and a larger strip, with goldfish pool and lawns, at the rear. If room permitted, a conifer tree or a clump of rhododendrons was a feature of the front garden. Such an architectural style was most charac-

STOCKBROKER'S TUDOR

WIMBLEDON TRANSITIONAL

Fig. 18

teristic of the south-western suburbs of London such as Wimbledon where upper middle-class houses abounded. As the style is half-way between the 'Stockbroker's Tudor' of the richest people, and the working-class dwellings on the Council estates, it may be called 'Wimbledon Transitional'.

Is this a pure style of architecture, or is it a mixed style?

Do you regard such houses as comfortable and convenient?

THE FUNCTIONAL STYLE OF HOUSE BUILDING

In the 1930's a number of original architects came to the sad conclusion that architecture was dead in the sense that it merely consisted of patching together elements of design from past styles, lacking originality or unity of purpose. Therefore, these architects felt, it was useless to continue hopeless efforts to revive the past but a completely new start must be made. Modern life, they argued, is governed by mechanical principles, and therefore the rules which hold good for the construction of machines must now be applied to architecture. A house, it is said, is a machine for living in; the success of a building is measured by its 'fitness for purpose'. Decoration and ornamentation are out of place; a building's effect on the beholder must depend on proportion and on its suitability to fill the role for which it was constructed.

Fig. 19 (top) shows small terrace houses at Hatfield New Town, in Hertfordshire, erected in 1955.

Why is so much emphasis placed on the outer walls and the roof?

If there is no decoration to give interest and variety to the buildings, differences in texture (i.e. roughness or smoothness, grain or pattern in surfaces) may achieve a like effect.

What differences of texture are noticeable on these houses?

Do you find the mixture of large and small windows a pleasing one?

Are there any recently-built functional dwellings or other buildings in your town? Draw some of them, and

MODERN HOUSING TYPES

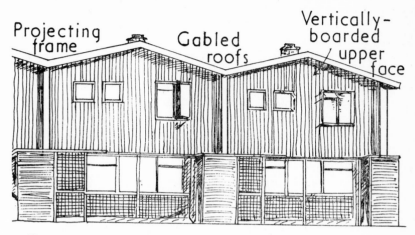

Projecting frame · Gabled roofs · Vertically-boarded upper face

TERRACE HOUSES HATFIELD NEW TOWN, 1955

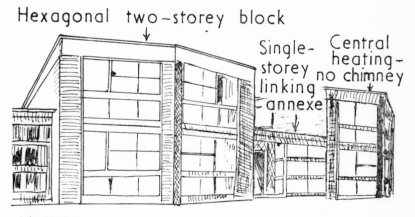

Hexagonal two-storey block · Single-storey linking annexe · Central heating-no chimney

LINKED ONE AND TWO-STOREY HOUSES SPAN ESTATE, WEYBRIDGE, SURREY

Fig. 19

discuss their use of textures, their constructional forms, etc.

In a gale, a number of houses in Hatfield New Town, rather similar to those shown, had their roofs ripped off.

Do you feel that there is a fault in design which makes for this sort of trouble?

Fig. 19 (bottom) shows houses in Oatlands Drive, Weybridge, Surrey, erected by Span Developments Ltd. in 1964. This building firm is noted for its experimental approach and its willingness to innovate.

Do you think that the hexagonal shape of the two storey houses is a convenient and artistic one?

The roofs are flat, supported by a very broad reinforced concrete beam called a dado-transom, supported on brick columns at each of the six corners. The framework of the house is thus completely revealed.

Do you find this a good method of construction, or would you prefer the framework to be concealed?

The two-storey hexagonal blocks are linked by annexes of one storey.

Do you think that this variation in height within a single house is a waste of space?

Do you feel that full-height windows in the living rooms tend to make them too cold in winter and too hot in very sunny weather, and also interfere with the privacy of the occupants?

Large cedar trees growing in the area before the houses were erected were left in place, even where they are very close to the houses.

Was this wise?

Do the trees add to or detract from the appearance of the estate?

LIVING IN FLATS (fig. 20)

The latest stages in the long history of living in cities have seen a reaction against the individualistic plan of living which ran riot in the space-consuming, detached and semi-detached, housing of the mid-twentieth century suburbs. The type of building which is now becoming increasingly common is the tall slab-block of flats or offices, the abode of a community rather than a collection of individual homes. The slab block is the shape which gives the greatest amount of floor space in relation to the ground which it covers. Thus, the slab block is in increasing favour for rehousing the occupants of formerly overcrowded areas, for at one and the same time groups of slab-blocks house very large numbers of people and give the maximum amount of light, fresh air and open recreational space for those who 'live high'.

Community dwellings are no novelty in England. In the middle of the nineteenth century, a number of philanthropists such as the American George Peabody sought to improve the living conditions of workers in congested towns by building blocks of flatlets; each approached by means of staircases and open galleries.

The idea of communal living in flats was revived in the 1930's a time when very solidly-built concrete buildings were in vogue.

Fig. 20 shows the Isokon Flats in Lawn Road, Hampstead, London, built in 1934. Twenty-two flatlets, four two-room and three studio flats are combined in this long and narrow building of reinforced concrete. It has five storeys, served by a staircase housed in the tower visible at the far end, and by the open galleries. It is a stark design, ignoring elegance or decorative additions.

> Do you find the contrast between white concrete and the blackness of the deep-shadowed galleries attractive?
> The design seems to call for a great number of right-angled junctions of walls, and yet hardly any of these in fact meet at right-angles.
> Do you think that this adds variety and beauty to the design?
> Every visible part of the building appears to be very thick-walled.
> Does this give an attractive sense of solidity and honesty, or do you find it grim and clumsy in appearance?

Fig. 20 also shows part of the Alton West Estate, Wandsworth, London, designed by the then London County Council's architects in 1955–9. On a sloping park-like site of 108 acres, nearly 2000 dwellings have been provided in 12-storey square towers, five ranges of buildings each containing five tiers of two-storey maisonettes, besides smaller terraces and groups of one to four storeys. Incorporated in the estate are two shopping centres, three primary schools, a community centre and a public library.

Does the Alton West Estate contain all the necessities for the 2000 families which inhabit it?

The buildings do not rest directly on the ground, but on the slim, reinforced concrete pillars around which the entire structure is balanced.

What uses can be made of the open spaces beneath the buildings?

Do you consider that it is dangerous for young children to live in the upper storeys?

If so, should these upper flats be allocated to older people?

If so, has this any disadvantages?

What is the evidence that the most distant of the three buildings is served by a lift?

Brightly-coloured plastic panels are often used for the cladding of these structures.

Do you think that the use of colour in this way is justified?

Do you consider that tall flats of this kind are dangerous in view of the possibility of extra-violent gales, outbreaks of fire, explosions of gas, or even earthquakes?

How can precautions be taken against such occurrences?

How do the Alton West flats compare with recently-erected blocks of flats in your own town?

Flats of this kind have a magnificent view but, if they become more numerous, will they harm the appearance of the town as a whole, and will not the view from one block be spoiled by other similar buildings rearing up in its vicinity?

ISOKON FLATS, HAMPSTEAD, LONDON 1934

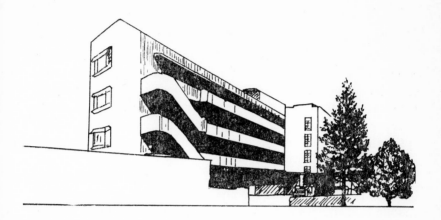

ALTON WEST ESTATE, WANDSWORTH, LONDON 1955-9

Fig. 20

3

THE TOWN AS A WORK PLACE

To know every part of a town in equal detail is an impossible and futile task. It is much better to gain an intimate acquaintance with a few separate pieces of the urban jigsaw, such as the town centre, an industrial quarter, a local shopping centre, a group of blocks of flats and a newly-erected housing estate. It is much better to study in great detail a few of the varied pieces which together make up an entire town than to try to cover the total area in a superficial way.

Having selected a small portion of the town for detailed study, let us 'plunge in at the deep end' by recording on a very large-scale base map the function of every plot of land. Take a tracing of part of an Ordnance Survey map on a scale of 50 inches or 25 inches to a mile, and showing every building and every plot-boundary. Go to the place and, by inspection, pencil upon the face of the map the function of every building and plot of land according to the following code:

M Manufacturing Industry
(M1 Extractive industry, such as mine or quarry; M2 Metal working; M3 Constructional engineering; M4 Electrical engineering; M5 Vehicle engineering; M6 Textile manufacture; M7 Food and drink manufacture or processing; M8 Paper and printing; M9, M10, M11 Other manufactures (not included in the above, which are characteristic of the locality.)
S Storage
(S1 Warehouse; S2 Builder's yard; S3 Coal depot or timber yard; S4 Petrol depot or garage; S5 Others.)
T Transport
(T1 Railway station; T2 Bus station; T3 Public car park; T4 Wharf or port installation; T5 Others.)
R Retail
(R1 Specialized shop belonging to a local firm; R2 Specialized shop or chain store belonging to a multiple firm; R3 General dealer; R4 Department store; R5

Market in a building; R6 Street market; R7 Catering establishment, including boarding houses, cafés, public houses and off-licenses; R8 Others.)

O Offices
(O1 Post Office; O2 Bank; O3 Insurance; O4 Legal; O5 House-agent, surveyor; O6 Others.)

P Public Buildings, Places of Assembly and Social Services Institutions
(P1 Central government offices; P2 Local government offices; P3 Place of worship; P4 School or College; P5 Hospital; P6 Cinema or theatre; P7 Club or hall; P8 Library; P9 Police station; P10 Others.)

X Open space
(X1 Park or the planted precinct of a public building; X2 Sports ground, golf course; X3 Reservoir, sewage farm; X4 Cemetery; X5 Allotments; X6 Nursery or market garden; X7 Residual fragment of farmland; X8 Woodland; X9 Derelict plot without buildings; X10 Derelict plot still occupied by ruined or disused buildings or other structures; X11 Others.)

D Dwellings
(D1 Residential hotel or boarding house; D2 Block of flats; D3 Terrace houses with front gardens; D4 Terrace houses without front gardens; D5 Detached and semi-detached villa or bungalow residence with garage or adequate garage space at side; D6 Detached and semi-detached villa or bungalow residence without garage or adequate garage space at side; D7 Large detached house in extensive grounds; D8 Dwelling above shop; D9 House used for professional purposes; D10 Empty house; D11 Others.)

This reference may be elaborated, if desired, in a number of ways:

The number of floors in each building may be shown by adding a second figure (following the functional figure) to show the number of floors, e.g. S13 represents a storage warehouse with three storeys.
The letter and the two following numbers may serve as the numerator of a fraction, whose denominator consists of three numbers. The first number may record the material of the roof as follows: **1** Slates; **2** Tiles; **3** Stone

Slabs; **4** Asbestos; **5** Corrugated Iron; **6** Concealed flat roof; **7** Others. The second number records the material of the walls as follows: **1** Stone; **2** Plaster overlying another material; **3** Brick; **4** Concrete; **5** Pebble-dash; **6** Weather-boarding; **7** Others. The third number may indicate the approximate period in which the building appears to have been erected, according to some scheme of building periods such as the following: **1** Pre-Tudor; **2** Tudor; **3** Seventeenth Century; **4** Georgian; **5** Early Victorian; **6** Late Victorian; **7** Post First World War (1918–39); **8** Post Second World War (1945–60); **9** Very recent.

AN EXAMPLE OF FRACTIONAL NOTATION: THREE STREETS IN GLOUCESTER

The result of this detailed mapping will be an almost complete record of the observable features of every observable plot of land shown on the Ordnance Survey map. It provides information relating to the function of each plot by means of the letters and figures in the numerator of the fraction. It gives details of the form of the building, including the structure, fabric and apparent age of the building, in the denominator of the fraction.

Fig. 21 shows the completed record of three streets in Gloucester. The fieldwork took more than an hour, and the map obtained is much too crowded to be comfortable or artistic, but it was well worth making because it made the fieldworkers very conscious of the variety and complexity of even a tiny portion of a town, and because this map provided the raw material from which a number of clear and elegant one-feature maps were created.

It will be seen that, wherever the map makers found several buildings of the same kind side by side, they merely recorded the appropriate fraction for one of them, and put after this within brackets the number of similar examples. Thus 136(5) means five similar dwellings with the same set of features common to all of them.

Test your knowledge of the code by looking at all the buildings on each side of, say, Hare Lane, and working out what each one is.

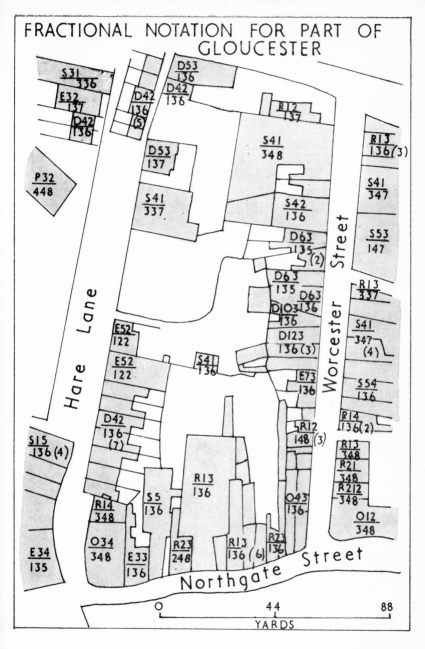

Fig. 21

Is this group of streets mainly residential, commercial or industrial? (In other words, which functional initial letter appears to be most common?)

Would you described this as an area of modern buildings or of older ones? (Look particularly at the last figure of the denominator.)

Is it an area of tall or of low buildings? (Look at the last figure of the numerator.)

A SERIES OF SINGLE-FEATURE MAPS

We may now proceed to draw a whole series of maps, each presenting in an uncongested way a single part of the total body of information which we collected on our field-work.

Suggested maps are:

An Industrial Map, made by tracing from our plot-by-plot survey all those buildings and plots with M as the first letter in the denominator. We could use the last letter in the denominator to separate the older industries from the new or rebuilt ones, and use a different colour for each.

A Shops Map, singling out all buildings with R in the numerator, using colours to distinguish different types of shop, guided by the second figure in the numerator.

A Social Services Map, showing all those places labelled from P4 to P10.

An Office Employment Map to show all buildings with O as the prefix of the numerator.

A Building Materials Map, calling on the information given in the first two figures of the denominator, covering materials of both walls and roof.

An Age of Buildings Map, perhaps the most difficult to make, because a good deal of guesswork is inevitable in arriving at the third figure in the denominator.

RECORDING THE CENTRAL BUSINESS DISTRICT OF A TOWN

The commercial core, or Central Business District of a town, has the largest claim to be an area for close study. Not only is it the hub of the town's manifold activities, but also the one where freedom to replan is often most restricted by the presence of historic buildings which no-one would wish to tear down.

The Central Business District, or C.B.D., may be defined as that part of the town centre which mainly consists of public buildings, shops and offices which serve the entire community rather than smaller sections of it. The Town Hall or Civic Centre, the Cathedral or principal parish church, the General Post Office, Central Public Library, Art Gallery and Museum, plus the branch or local headquarters of banks, insurance and building societies, a few large departmental stores and a number of high-class specialized shops and restaurants are all characteristic features of the Central Business District, but of no other part of the town. Multi-storied offices and shops are common, but dwelling-houses are rare. Parked cars are little in evidence, but large numbers of pedestrians throng every road-crossing, so that the creation of traffic-free shopping precincts is often called for.

Signs that the edges of the Central Business District are being reached, as we progress outwards from the town centre, are the growing numbers of buildings typical of the Inner Zone, such as storage warehouses, servicing workshops, garages and car dealers, former dwellings converted into lawyers' and dealers' offices, and the appearance of supermarkets and miscellaneous small shops, including cut-price grocers, dealers in second-hand goods and transport cafés. This area will usually contain the main railway and bus stations, postal sorting offices and transport depots. Congested streets of obsolete housing, partially replaced by blocks of recent and older flats, become more and more evident, proclaiming the Inner Zone to be a 'twilight zone', or one on which 'urban blight' has visibly laid its hand with the result that rebuilding and even the realignment of streets will often be taking place.

DELIMITING THE CENTRAL BUSINESS DISTRICT

In order to ascertain the extent and shape of the Central Business District by fieldwork methods, a base map on a scale of 50 inches or 25 inches to a mile is required, together with two lists appropriate to the town to be studied. The first list is one of buildings special to the C.B.D., the other is of buildings which are more appropriate to the Inner Zone. By inspection, mark 'C' on every building which has one or more floors devoted to

Central Business District uses, and 'X' on buildings and plots whose use relegates them to the Inner Zone. Many buildings, where there is doubt about which letter to insert, will not be marked with either letter.

When all streets around the town centre have been inspected, a continuous line is drawn on the map to enclose the area which is dominated by the C symbol and to exclude those areas where the X symbol is especially common. The course of this line must be checked on a second visit to the central parts of the town, with particular attention to relative heights of buildings. Often a sharp difference in the relative heights of buildings, or in the care and expense lavished on their frontages, may be observable at the limits of the C.B.D.

GLOUCESTER'S C.B.D.

Fig. 22 shows a stage in delimiting Gloucester's C.B.D. Most buildings along Westgate Street have been labelled C or X, and a line has been drawn to separate the main concentration of the one letter from that of the other. Similar lines will be drawn across adjacent streets and their ends linked to form a continuous line enclosing the city's hub.

What buildings in Westgate Street are unlikely to be represented in any other part of Gloucester?

How many multiple stores or branches of very large chains of shops are to be found in Westgate Street?

What are the main differences between the left-hand and the right-hand sides of Westgate Street?

Why do you think one shoe shop is labelled C while others have no letter?

Why are butchers' shops, fish-and-chip shops and fruit shops usually rare in the C.B.D. of a town?

THE C.B.D. IN ELEVATION

The activities of the C.B.D. should be recorded in elevation as well as in plan, because it so largely consists of multi-storeyed buildings whose uses may differ from one floor to another.

In preparation for a record of the elevation of buildings in Northgate, Gloucester, the pages of a field notebook were ruled with horizontal lines, no less in number than there are storeys in the buildings facing the street. Additional horizontal lines were

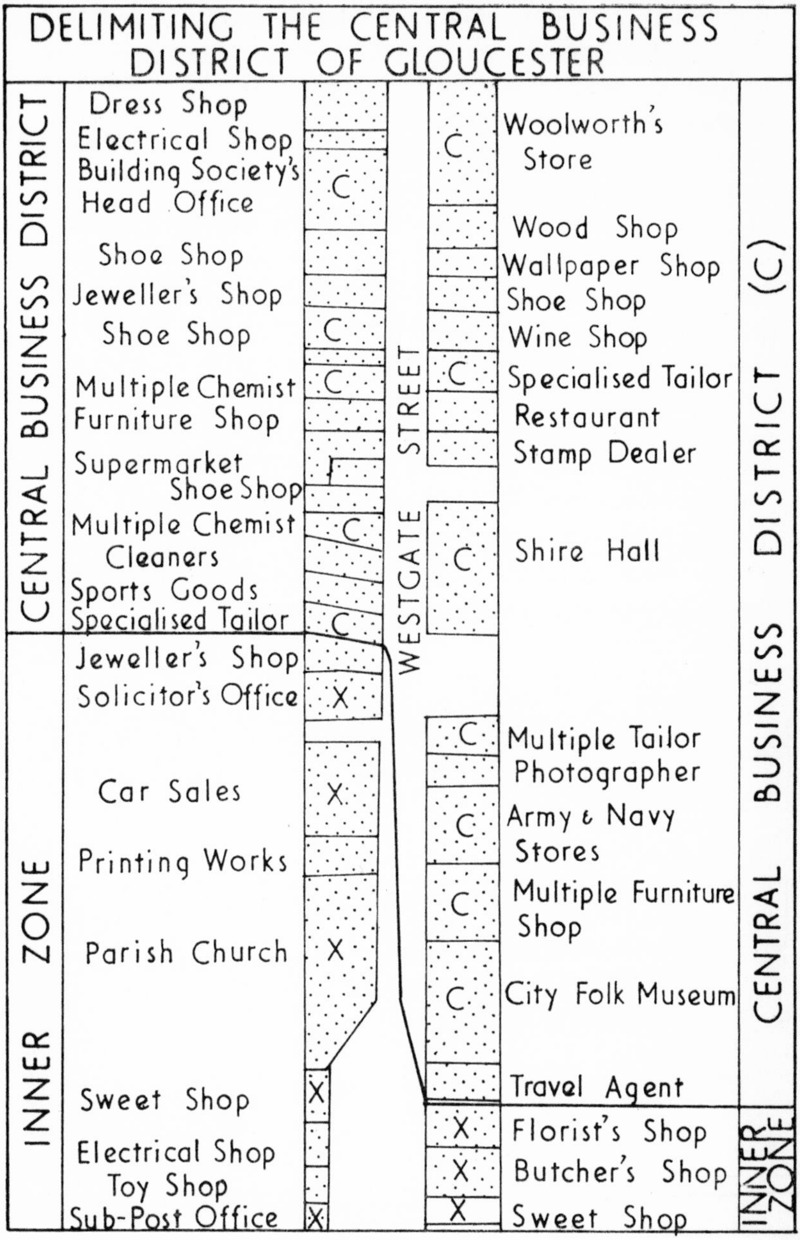

DELIMITING THE CENTRAL BUSINESS DISTRICT OF GLOUCESTER

CENTRAL BUSINESS DISTRICT / INNER ZONE		WESTGATE STREET		CENTRAL BUSINESS DISTRICT (C) / INNER ZONE
CENTRAL BUSINESS DISTRICT	Dress Shop Electrical Shop Building Society's Head Office	C	C	Woolworth's Store
	Shoe Shop Jeweller's Shop Shoe Shop	C		Wood Shop Wallpaper Shop Shoe Shop Wine Shop
	Multiple Chemist Furniture Shop	C	C	Specialised Tailor Restaurant Stamp Dealer
	Supermarket Shoe Shop			
	Multiple Chemist Cleaners	C	C	Shire Hall
	Sports Goods Specialised Tailor	C		
INNER ZONE	Jeweller's Shop Solicitor's Office	X		
			C	Multiple Tailor Photographer
	Car Sales	X	C	Army & Navy Stores
	Printing Works		C	Multiple Furniture Shop
	Parish Church	X	C	City Folk Museum
				Travel Agent
	Sweet Shop	X	X	Florist's Shop
	Electrical Shop Toy Shop		X	Butcher's Shop
	Sub-Post Office	X	X	Sweet Shop

Right column labels: **CENTRAL BUSINESS DISTRICT (C)** / **CENTRAL BUSINESS DISTRICT** / **INNER ZONE**

Fig. 22

61

added, to enable information gathered about building materials and the age of buildings to be inserted (Fig. 23).

Along the bottom of the notebook page, a line was marked off to scale to represent the frontage lines of individual buildings along one side of the street. Vertical lines were drawn through the points of subdivision, to create a series of small compartments into which symbols or abbreviated words were inserted to indicate the use to which every part of the building was put. It often became necessary to inspect name-plates on doorways, signs in upper windows, and to make discreet personal enquiries before the use of upper-storey rooms could be recorded. The results were presented in the form of a series of maps. One showed ground floor uses only; a second showed first floor uses and a third summarized the uses of second and higher floors where they existed. An additional map (Fig. 24) showed the number of storeys in each building in Central Gloucester.

ELEVATION OF BUILDINGS IN NORTH GATE ST., GLOUCESTER

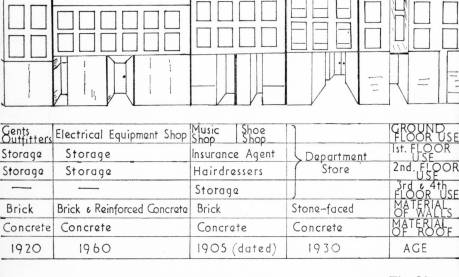

Gents Outfitters	Electrical Equipment Shop	Music Shop	Shoe Shop	Department Store	GROUND FLOOR USE
Storage	Storage	Insurance Agent			1st. FLOOR USE
Storage	Storage	Hairdressers			2nd. FLOOR USE
—	—	Storage			3rd & 4th FLOOR USE
Brick	Brick & Reinforced Concrete	Brick		Stone–faced	MATERIAL OF WALLS
Concrete	Concrete	Concrete		Concrete	MATERIAL OF ROOF
1920	1960	1905 (dated)		1930	AGE

Fig. 23

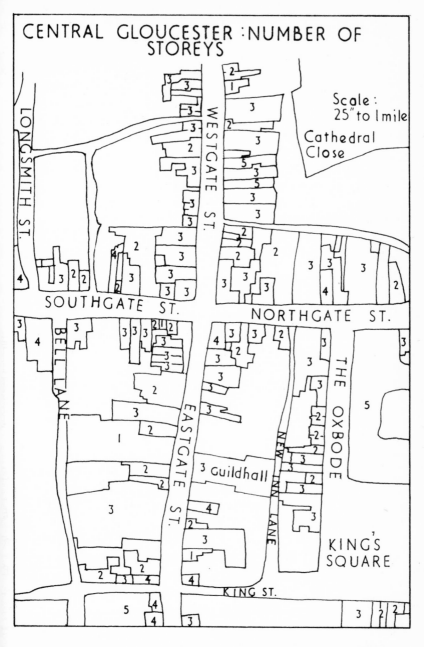

Fig. 24

63

Which buildings in Northgate Street, Gloucester, may be designated single-purpose buildings, and which have mixed uses?

Describe the differences between the frontages of the Northgate Street buildings.

What can be done to provide the maximum amount of shop-window space if the frontage is of limited length?

What proportion of the total floor space, assuming all the buildings to be of the same depth, appears to be devoted to shopping, how much to storage, and how much to services of all kinds?

Are Gloucester's tallest buildings in the heart of the town or somewhat removed from it?

Which of the four principal streets of Gloucester has the largest proportion of tall buildings?

Is there much harmony in the heights of buildings along the streets of Gloucester?

Are there any suitable places left where a group of multi-storey buildings might be erected?

THE TWILIGHT ZONE OF A TOWN

Immediately surrounding the centres of most large towns is a girdle of mixed building, obsolete, confused and often decayed, known as the Inner Zone or sometimes as the Twilight Zone. This blighted area presents a town planning problem huge in scale and very far from solution.

Twilight houses, together with slums, form one of the threads in the confused pattern. Many are nineteenth century workers' dwellings, built in tightly packed terraces to enable them to be let at low rents at a time when land was dear, and built low to satisfy Victorian local bye-laws severely limiting the heights of houses. But they present more than a problem of straightforward building.

It was a feature of their growth that they were entangled in a web of other and often quite inappropriate uses, e.g. railways and railway sidings, warehouses, small industries and craftsmen's workshops, old canals and curious backyards. Not only are the houses decayed, but the whole layout of streets is out-of-date. Above all, they lack open space.

Another feature of twilight zones is the way in which buildings are often used for purposes other than those for which they were built. Spacious Victorian houses are split up into flatlets, or have shop fronts added to them. Other shops have their fronts boarded up so that they may be used as warehouses, and obsolete chapels may become furniture stores. Many buildings stand empty, and when they become unsafe through decay, they may be cleared away to leave unsightly spaces like gaps in a row of bad teeth.

CHANGES IN USE OF BUILDINGS

It is helpful to make a map to show changes in the use of buildings. It is necessary to consult in a Public Library an out-of-date copy of a street directory, which states the names of the occupants of the buildings and often the occupations in which they engaged, at some past date.

Fig. 25 shows in italics the uses of buildings in Clarence Street, Gloucester, as recorded in a 1920 directory and as they were observed to be used in 1967.

What change has taken place in the general character of Clarence Street since 1920?

In what types of buildings has there been the greatest degree of change?

King William IV, Queen Victoria's predecessor, was Duke of Clarence before his accession.

What does this suggest as a possible date for the first building in Clarence Street?

Why was the café set up in the position which it now occupies?

Fig. 26 shows Gloucester's Twilight Zone in its entirety.

To what extent can be shaded areas regarded as an almost continuous zone around the Central Business District?

Many empty buildings are found in the vicinity of the docks.

What does this suggest about the present-day prosperity of the docks?

Queen Victoria ruled from 1837 to 1901; her uncle, George IV, was at one time Prince Regent and the Battle of Alma took place during the Crimean War from 1853–6.

What does this suggest about the age of the twilight zone housing?

CHANGES OF USE OF BUILDINGS IN CLARENCE STREET, GLOUCESTER 1920-67

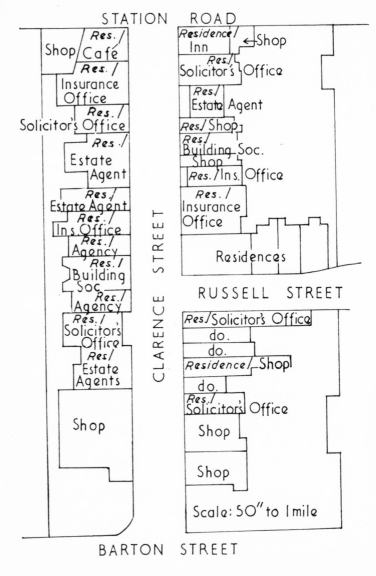

Fig. 25

What mode of transport seems to be most closely associated with the building of this now obsolete housing?

Why is it that some railway stations have lately passed out of use?

THE REBUILDING OF THE INNER ZONES OF TOWNS

In England and Wales there are about 17 million houses, of which nearly half were built before 1920. Their average age is fifty-six years. It follows that between three and five million houses either need replacement or radical improvement. Most of the obsolete houses, together with the slums, form a large part of the twilight areas girdling the city centres. But it is just in these areas where the difficulties of replacement are most acute.

The cost of land in such areas is very high because of their proximity to the city centres, and the presence of industrial buildings within them. The land is also divided into small parcels in the hands of a great number of owners, many of them far from rich. It is only the city councils who can tackle redevelopment, and this is both time-consuming and very costly: for comprehensive rebuilding demands ownership of large areas, otherwise the orderly replanning of streets and spaces is not practicable. A major cost arises from the need to devote considerable areas of land previously occupied by buildings to open spaces, new and better roads and schools. For this reason, it is found that when nine acres are cleared of dwellings, only five of them are available for the new ones. Furthermore, it is necessary to build new houses at a much lower density of people to the acre. Perhaps half the people have to be rehoused elsewhere, so there is a problem of overspill as well as of rehousing on the spot.

The replacement of terraced houses by tall blocks of flats is only a partial solution to the problem of the twilight zones. In Britain, high building is considerably more costly than building two-storey houses. This will probably change as the building industry improves its methods, but at the moment multi-storey buildings may be 40 per cent more costly in London and up to 70 per cent more costly in the provinces. It is dangerous to produce the most expensive forms of housing for the people who may be least able to afford the rent.

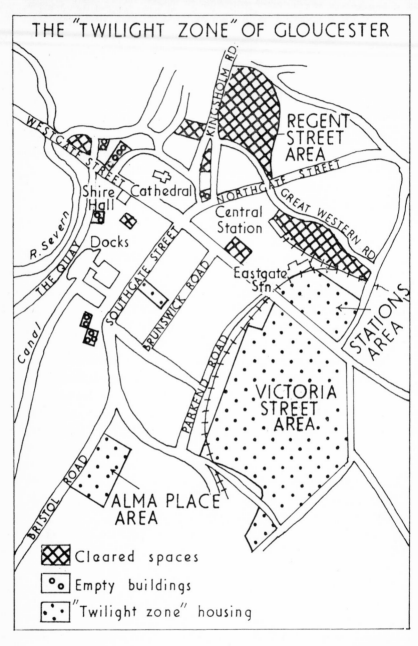

THE "TWILIGHT ZONE" OF GLOUCESTER

REGENT STREET AREA

WESTGATE STREET

KINGSHOLM RD.

NORTHGATE STREET

Shire Hall

Cathedral

Central Station

GREAT WESTERN RD

R. Severn

THE QUAY

Docks

Eastgate Stn.

SOUTHGATE STREET

BRUNSWICK ROAD

Canal

PARKEND ROAD

STATIONS AREA

VICTORIA STREET AREA.

BRISTOL ROAD

ALMA PLACE AREA

⬛ Cleared spaces

°₀° Empty buildings

∴ "Twilight zone" housing

Fig. 26

There are real social problems created by rehousing in high flats. With higher buildings, private gardens begin to be eliminated; for families with young children this can be a serious loss. Parents whose children play in the rooms of tall flats may fear that they may fall into the streets, or have an accident in the lift. Many rehoused people, particularly the old, miss the busy, congested, vital character of the little streets, shops and markets which have been demolished, and suffer from loneliness and the feeling that they cannot fit into the new mode of living.

TOO FEW OR TOO MANY PEOPLE PER ACRE?

In the older areas of towns there are striking differences between one area and another in the present density of population. Both extremes, over-congestion and under-use of space, are equally bad. In some slum areas in the past, such as the Gorbals in Glasgow, the density could reach as high as 1500 people per acre. There is nothing like this today, but densities of 300–400 people per acre are still to be found in major cities. A reasonable average figure is 136 per square mile. At the other extreme, many areas with houses standing in extensive gardens, and built in the days of large Victorian households with many children and even more domestic servants, are now under-occupied. Both extremes are undesirable, and call urgently for replanning.

It is interesting to take two areas of similar extent, and write upon each building, as shown on the map, the number of people in each house. (If this is not known through personal acquaintance, it is possible to find out the number of adults above the age of 21 living in each building by consulting the Electoral Registers which are often available on request at Post Offices and Town Halls.) This has been done for two contrasted areas in Gloucester, the over-congested Clapham area and the under-occupied Kingsholm area (Fig. 27).

How many people live in Sweetbriar Street?

Which has most inhabitants, Columbia Street or Suffolk Street?

Is there any relationship between number of people and size of house in either Clapham or Kingsholm area?

Are the street patterns of the two areas suitable for safe and speedy transport?

69

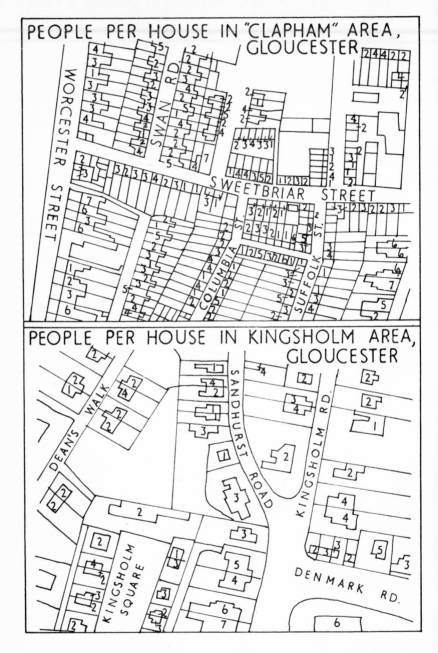

Fig. 27

THE PROGRESS OF URBAN REPLACEMENT IN GLOUCESTER

Fig. 28 was made in the course of an hour's walk in Gloucester, searching for buildings which were new or rebuilt over the past five years.

Is most of the rebuilding in the Central Business District in the Inner Zone or in the suburbs?

Is the new building evenly distributed over the town or is it restricted to certain parts?

If so, what are these parts, and how do you account for the selection of these to contain its newest developments?

Is there much new industrial building in Gloucester? What other types of building appear to be favoured?

What appears to be the policy of the Governmental and civic offices in regard to the siting of new buildings for their own use?

Have the four main streets witnessed many changes over the past five years?

Which of the streets has changed most?

AN INDUSTRIAL SURVEY OF AN AREA

The method of comprehensive survey using the fractional notation, outlined in the early pages of this chapter, can well be applied to the chief industrial districts of the town.

To make a map showing the overall pattern of the location of industry within the town, trace from a 6-inch or 2½ inch Ordnance Survey Map the positions of all factories, mines, quarries and waste tips, together with the roads, navigable waterways and railways which serve them. This will be the prelude to studies of individual enterprises.

A FACTORY VISIT

Visit a representative factory or works from each of the main groups to be found within the town. Make up your mind before you start that your main purpose must be not so much to observe the processes which are carried on there, but to ascertain so far as possible the factors which have caused the industry to

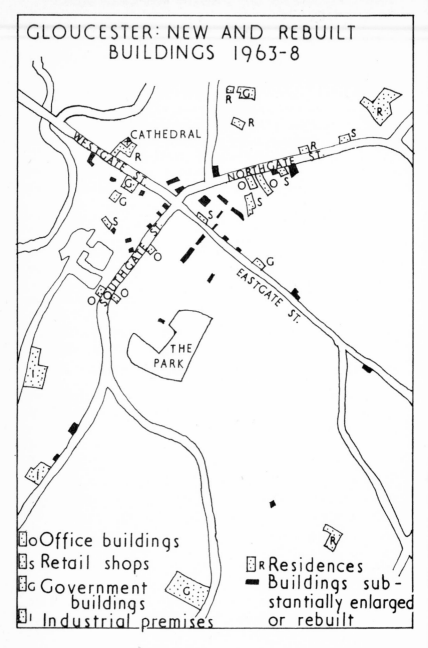

GLOUCESTER: NEW AND REBUILT BUILDINGS 1963-8

CATHEDRAL

WESTGATE ST.

NORTHGATE ST.

SOUTHGATE ST.

EASTGATE ST.

THE PARK

Office buildings
Retail shops
Government buildings
Industrial premises

Residences
Buildings sub-stantially enlarged or rebuilt

Fig. 28

be sited at that particular place. The following are headings under which a written account may be drawn up, accompanied by a sketch-plan of the layout of the constituent parts of the enterprise.

Sources of raw materials. These may be local, and of the type which tie industries closely to their areas of production, as in cement-making, sugar-beet refining or brick-making. Alternatively, they may be imported by ship, railway or road.

Availability of water supplies. Many industries require exceptionally large supplies for cooling, etc. and may be located beside a large river or on the sea, or may require a supply of very soft water to reduce the cost of defurring boilers.

Power supplies. These may well have changed during the history of a long-established industry. An Oxford-shire woollen mill may originally have been sited near a waterfall which provided power to turn the mill-wheels, and not far from a pit where Fuller's Earth was dug for cleansing the cloth before dying, and near the sheep pastures of the Cotswolds. The industry continues in this location, even though the mill may now be run by electric power and use Australian wool.

Labour supply. Often an industry may have become established because of the gap left by the decline of other occupations in the area, or because the closing of a war-time shell-filling factory made workers and premises available. Once an industry has become well-established, other firms may erect factories to draw on the experienced labour force available in the area, or to draw advantage from the reputation of the place for a certain product, e.g. Sheffield for special varieties of steel.

Availability of a market for finished products. An increasing number of industries are becoming market-orientated. The market may be a local one, as when a large town requires a factory making electric light bulbs, potato crisps or mineral waters in its vicinity, or it may depend on good communication with other parts of Britain or export markets.

Availability of communications. Most industries depend for their continuance on their ability to marshal raw materials and work-people, and to distribute their finished products cheaply and rapidly. The physical character of the surrounding countryside may well contribute to this.

Availability of suitable land. Many factories, particularly those powered by electricity or having very heavy equipment, need an area of flat, relatively cheap land not zoned for agricultural purposes.

Facility for disposal of waste products may well be a decisive factor in the choice of a river-side site downstream from a large town, or a site on drained marshland remote from settlements to which the waste may be offensive in smell or appearance.

Availability of capital. No industrial works can begin before capital has been laid down to buy land, erect suitable buildings and install plant. Ascertain whether local capital was available for investment and, if outside capital was called for, why such an enterprise in that particular place was considered a good investment.

SHOPPING IN A TOWN

The Central Business District is unable, on its own account, to provide services for the entire population of any but the smallest towns. The organization of the retail distribution of food and other consumer goods, and the provision of social and cultural services for a very large population is beyond the competence of the central core. Only for the most centralized services does the core serve and dominate the whole built-up area. A wide range of services, catering for all of the day-to-day needs and many of the less frequent needs of the population are provided by shopping and service centres located within the residential areas. It is necessary in the field study of a town to enquire into the nature, location and varied importance of such centres.

The least important of these shopping and service centres is the 'neighbourhood group' of shops, often on a street-corner in the older residential suburbs. It usually consists of a general store specializing in grocery, accompanied by two or three others which perform either one or a combination of the following – greengrocery, newspapers, stationery, tobacco and confectionery.

Many shops in the street corner group may be seen to be converted private dwellings, to which a shop-front has been added.

THE SUBURBAN SERVICE CENTRE

The second type is the suburban service centre, a cluster of shops, banks and a cinema or restaurant which satisfy most of the needs of a suburb in much the same way as the Central Business District services the town as a whole.

In mapping a service centre, letters or colours are inserted on a large-scale map according to a scheme of classification such as the following:

A Bank
B Post Office
C Chain store
D Clothing, knitting wool, draper's or tailor's shop
E Furniture, carpet, china or glass shop
F Food shop
G Radio, television, gramophone or music shop
H Chemist's or photographic equipment shop
J Cinema or theatre
K Other shop, not in the above categories

An attempt should be made to find out the extent of the area from which the service centre draws its customers. This may begin with listing those streets which are easily accessible to the centre by a frequent bus service. This information must be supplemented by local knowledge of where housewives are accustomed to make their shopping visits.

Fig. 29 shows by means of a dot the addresses of all persons using a new shopping centre at the Elephant and Castle in South London. It will be seen that almost all the shoppers come from within a mile's radius. Fig. 30 shows the location of this shopping centre and also of its competitors.

Is there any evidence that customers are by-passing shopping centres near their homes in order to shop at the Elephant and Castle?
What is the maximum distance from which customers travel?

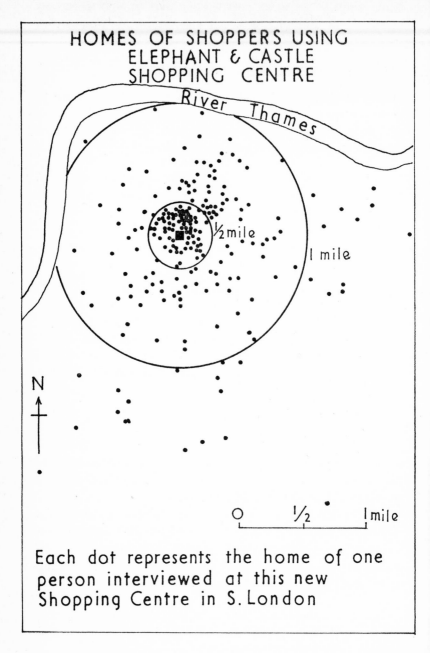

HOMES OF SHOPPERS USING
ELEPHANT & CASTLE
SHOPPING CENTRE

River Thames

½mile

I mile

N

O   ½   I mile

Each dot represents the home of one
person interviewed at this new
Shopping Centre in S. London

Fig. 29

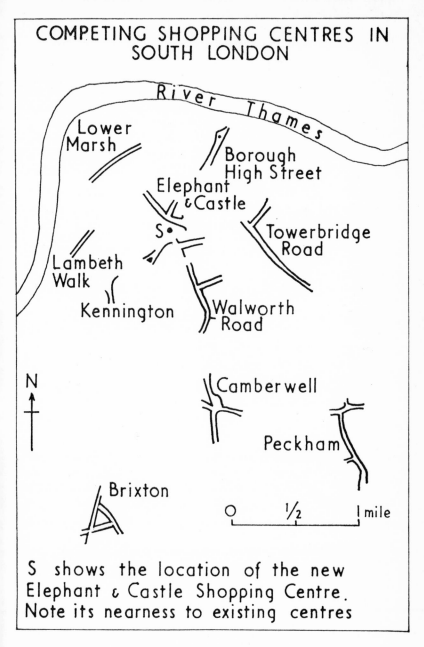

COMPETING SHOPPING CENTRES IN SOUTH LONDON

S shows the location of the new Elephant & Castle Shopping Centre. Note its nearness to existing centres

Fig. 30

THE RANKING OF SHOPPING CENTRES

Visit a number of local shopping centres and ascertain for each one whether or not it contains certain features which contribute to a high place in the ranking of shopping centres, from the most humble to the most important. A point may be awarded for each of the features mentioned below which is present; the total number of points gained by each centre is a measure of the range and quality which it possesses as a shopping and service centre. The following scheme of ranking is appropriate to the largest towns: it needs adjustment to enable it to fit smaller towns.

Grade D centre. A mere group of shops serving a small group of neighbouring streets.

Grade C−. A group of shops including a Woolworth's store.

Grade C. The combination of a Woolworth's store, a main post office and at least three banks.

Grade C+. All those in C, with the addition of chain tailors' shops, shoe shops, and also insurance offices.

Grade B. All the above with the addition of a Marks & Spencer store, or British Home Stores, or a departmental store of comparable size, or a chain jewellery store or a number of fashion-clothing shops.

Grade A. A major shopping centre with several competing department stores, and with a market, a college of technical or further education and a local government headquarters or Town Hall.

THE SPACING OF SERVICE CENTRES

It is important to study, not only what services and facilities are available in a town, but how conveniently they are spaced out over the area which it covers. It is common to find shopping centres which are well laid out with fine shops, but lack customers because the centre is badly placed, so that potential customers are put off by a long and inconvenient journey to reach the shops. Other shopping centres lack their due share of customers because these have the choice of two or more centres equally close at hand.

To study the spacing of shopping-service centres, lay tracing paper over a medium scale map, such as the 6 inch Ordnance Survey map, on which dots have been placed to mark the hub of each shopping centre (Fig. 31). Draw on the tracing paper straight lines from every shopping centre to all its immediate neighbours. Measure each line and insert the distance over it. In Fig. 31, this has been begun: complete the map. Complete also the histogram below the map to show the number of times each particular distance is repeated. Show the number of occurences along the vertical axis and the distances themselves along the horizontal axis.

What is the most frequent distance between adjacent shopping centres in S.E. London?

How do the outer suburbs differ from the inner suburbs in the spacing of their centres?

Mark the midpoint of each inter-centre line. Join midpoints to form polygons of various shapes and sizes, each with a single shopping-service centre at or near its centre. These are shown as dotted lines in Fig. 32. The result is a mesh or network of service-territories, each of which may be regarded as dependent upon its centre. Ideally, the pattern should be one of small regular hexagons; figures with the best packing power.

Do any of the actual polygons show projections? These draw attention to the extensions of one shopping centre's area into the territory of another.

Are there any very compact and small polygons? These denote areas nearer Central London where, over the years, shopping and service centres are closely and evenly spaced.

Are there any very large polygons, with very distorted shapes, particularly in the newer and outer suburbs where processes of adjustment are incomplete?

Are there any polygons whose hubs are far removed from the geometrical centres?

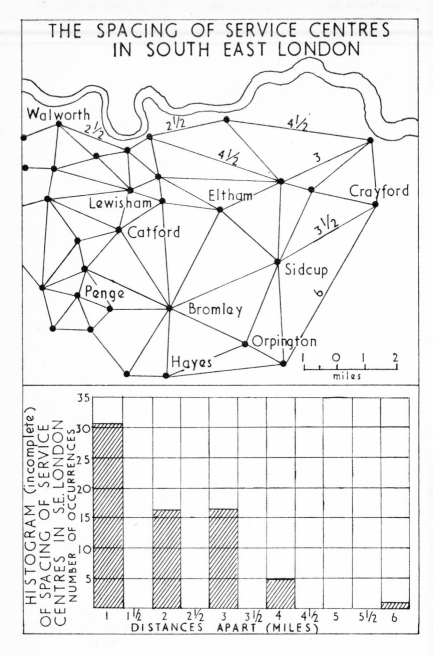

Fig. 31

THE SPACING OF MAJOR SHOPPING CENTRES

Shopping centres not only vary greatly in size, but also in the type and quality of the shops which they contain. The smallest shopping centres consist merely of shops selling the sort of food-stuffs which families need to buy regularly and frequently, and are usually near at hand. By contrast, there are important shopping centres which consist largely of large shops having vast displays of furniture, clothing and fancy goods, which people visit when they want as wide a choice of these lines as possible. Major shopping centres are also focal points for enter-tainment as well as shopping: at night they are 'bright light' districts where people tend to congregate to admire the window displays in the large stores, to visit the cinema or theatre and to have a meal or drink in a smart restaurant or inn. Each major centre in Greater London serves a large district in much the same way as the West End of London serves the conurbation as a whole.

Fig. 33 shows the major shopping or service centres in South-East London. To study the spacing of these centres, draw a line from each suburb whose centre is marked by a dot, to the nearest major shopping centre, marked by a larger dot with a circle round it. Then complete a histogram, similar to the one already begun beneath the map, to show the range of distances which South-East London's people need to travel in order to reach a shopping centre, and also the most common of the distances travelled.

Also, a rather rough map of the area which each major shopping centre serves may be obtained by a method similar to that used for Fig. 32. Join up each centre to its nearest neigh-bours by means of a thin straight line. Find the mid-point of each line, and join each to its immediate neighbours among the mid-points to obtain a series of six-sided figures which correspond to the theoretical areas each centre serves, assuming that the drawing powers of all centres are equal to one another.

SHOPPING STREET STUDIES

Any shopping street of twenty or more shops provides scope for many interesting field studies. Problems which arise in shop-ping streets are investigated by trained business consultants and

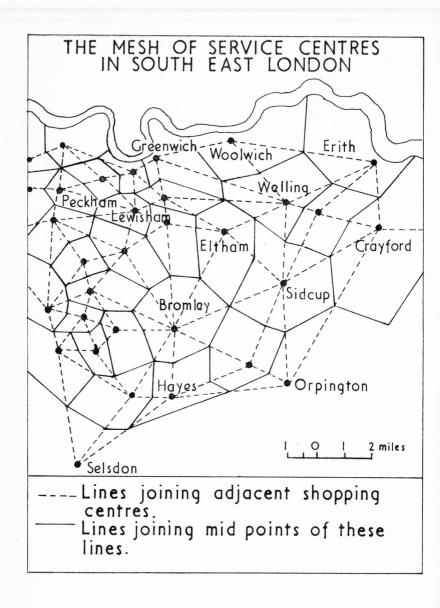

THE MESH OF SERVICE CENTRES
IN SOUTH EAST LONDON

Greenwich
Woolwich
Erith
Welling
Peckham
Lewisham
Eltham
Crayford
Sidcup
Bromley
Hayes
Orpington
Selsdon

1 O 1 2 miles

- - - - Lines joining adjacent shopping
centres.
——— Lines joining mid points of these
lines.

Fig. 32

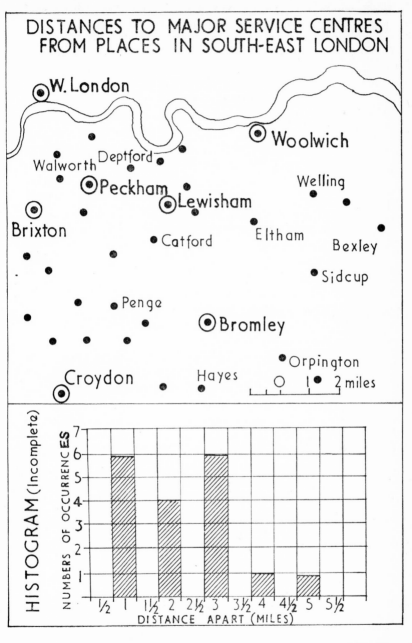

DISTANCES TO MAJOR SERVICE CENTRES FROM PLACES IN SOUTH-EAST LONDON

HISTOGRAM (Incomplete)

Fig. 33

investigators, but any of us may emulate some of the detective work which these undertake to find out why some shops have booming success while others languish for lack of customers.

Allocate the shops along a street to a small number of groups according to what they sell, and calculate the proportions of each. A complicated form of grouping is into Categories A–K as set out on pp. 75–8. A simpler grouping is into three classes – Food and common necessities, less frequent requirements, occasional requirements. Another grouping is into service shops, food and drink, clothing and other types.

Find out the approximate frontage of each shop by measurement on an Ordnance Survey map on a scale of 50 inches or 25 inches to a mile, or by pacing.

From the information assembled for this and the previous exercise, work out the total frontage of the shops in each of the classification groups indicated above.

Repeat these two investigations for another shopping street in another part of the town.

Compare the results obtained, and seek to account for the differences.

Two shops with a somewhat specialized trade, such as television and wireless shops or furnishing stores, are sometimes found very close to one another, and are therefore highly competitive.

Record over a period of time the measures taken by each shop to increase its share of the trade, such as striking window displays, price cutting, special offers and advertising campaigns.

For sample periods record the number of customers who enter each of the competing shops.

Seek to account for observed differences.

Record any evidence that shops on one side of a street, or in one part only of the street, appear to have more customers and to do more trade than the remainder.

Seek possible explanations for this. These may be looked for in such factors as accessibility, nearness to parking space, and propinquity to other prosperous concerns so that the prosperity of the one, as it were, 'rubs off' on its neighbours.

The presence of certain luxury-goods shops, such as

furriers, camera and photographic supplies dealers and jewellers is sometimes said to be indicative of a relatively prosperous shopping area.

Assess the truth of this generalization by a comparison of two streets, one with several shops of this type and the other lacking them.

It is sometimes said that the presence of a branch of a well-known multiple booksellers' and stationers' firm signifies the existence of a large public interest in high-class reading.

Is this true of any branch which you have come across?

It is sometimes said that a Marks & Spencer store signifies a possible market of at least 30,000 people.

Is this likely to be true of a branch which you have encountered?

Imagine that one or two adjacent shops in a local shopping street can be demolished, and replaced by the entrance to a shopping precinct consisting of eight shops.

What premises would you choose to replace by this precinct, and what eight shops would it be most profitable to set around the precinct, having regard to what shops are already to be found in its vicinity?

Note any shopping street which has a constriction, such as a narrow bridge.

Observe the extent to which shoppers tend to frequent the shops on one side or other of the constriction and avoid passing it.

To what extent do two newsagents' shops, on opposite sides of the constriction, tend to limit their delivery areas to one side of it or the other?

DO WE GET THE SHOPPING CENTRES WE WANT?

Usually, shopping centres have developed gradually, additions have been made in the course of years, and many shops have changed their uses many times. It is only by accident that the sorts of shops which customers really want are represented in any shopping parade. Now and again, a new shopping centre which was constructed all at one time is to be found, such as Leegate in South London, but even here the shops were built and then let to the first comers who were willing to pay the rent, whether or not they were those who stocked the range of goods which the people of Lee hope to find in these shops. Very rarely, a firm of shop developers consults customers by means of house-to-house enquiries to find what they really expect of a shopping centre before starting to plan and build one. Fryern Arcade in Chandler's Ford, a community of 15,000 people just outside Southampton, is the result of planning the sort of centre the shoppers wanted.

What are your own ideas about the sort of shopping centre a place of this size should have?

Are your ideas shared by great numbers of people? Answer the questions below and then see to what extent your answers agree with those of the people of this Hampshire community.

Should shopping be under cover?

Should a free parking place form part of the shopping centre?

How many cars should it be able to hold at one time?

For which of the following amenities should space be found? Public telephones, public lavatories, bench seats, a pram rail, a dog rail, children's playground.

Should a restaurant be included? Indoor, outdoor or partly both?

Obviously a food shop, a shoe shop and clothing shops should be included, but which is the next most essential?

Which of the following do you think would be considered essential by more than half the people? Radio, T.V. and electrical shop, pet shop, jewellery shop, furrier, betting shop, laundrette, dry cleaners.

Should shops pay a set annual rent or should they pay a percentage of their turnover?

If the latter, what would be a reasonable percentage to pay?

Should shops be all on one level, or on more than one to ensure greater compactness?

Where should cars be parked— in the centre of a U-shaped shopping centre, outside the centre and therefore out of sight, or on ground level below shops on the first floor?

Should cars be entirely separated from shoppers?

THE TOWN AS A PLACE FOR LIVING

4

There was a time when towns were small, and meant a great deal to their inhabitants. To the people of ancient Rome, the city was a real person. They knew the legends of its miraculous foundation by two children, Romulus and Remus, who were laid on a hillside to die, but were suckled by a she-wolf. Rome was founded by legendary heroes, and time was reckoned from the date of its foundation in 753 B.C. according to the later Christian system of dating all events from the birth of Jesus Christ.

While towns remained small, it was possible to see their essential functions by a single glance at their ground plans. Form grew out of function, a town might be a market-town, a river-bridge town, a cross-roads town or a town on a harbour; it was this and little more besides.

Unfortunately, in the haste of development since the Industrial Revolution, many of our towns have ceased to be the attractive and comprehensible places for living which they might be. Our towns tend to be a collection of villages and hamlets thrown together into a town by the needs of modern industry. They are huge and shapeless. We feel ourselves unable to check their ceaseless advance across the landscape. We feel ourselves powerless in the face of these monsters which spread across the countryside only to join each other's sprawling fringes. Towns flow together to form a conurbation, an ugly word for a nasty thing.

THE OVERALL VIEW OF A TOWN

Our ancestors on approaching a town were able to recognize it by its distant skyline, which was distinctive and individual to that town. Part of that impact depended on the town's colour, which depended on the predominant building materials. An East Anglian town was composed of warm red brick viewed against a foreground of arable land; a Cheshire town bore a magpie aspect of elaborate black timbering infilled with whitewashed plaster, seen against a foreground of green pastures. The impact also depended on the predominance of one or two large buildings near the centre, the silhouette of a Castle or Cathedral town, the spire of a parish church, or the tall square block of a maltings or brewery beside a river quay.

Urban spread in the last century has made the profile in any case difficult to spot, and the placing of tall buildings almost indiscriminately over the face of the town has been an even more serious threat to recognition and a sense of uniqueness. To take a walk from the centre of a town towards one or other of the outer suburbs is to reveal the way in which, as the town has grown, the layout and design of its constituent parts has changed. Everyone can tell roughly the point at which the town centre, with its recognizable forms and functions, is left and we pass into the mechanical repetition of by-law terraced houses of 1860–1918. This in turn gives place to the housing estates, some erected by local authorities and others by private builders, which have been the mark of the years since 1918.

MAKING AN URBAN TRANSECT

The traverse method is the best way of setting down the broad differences within the land occupied by a town. The traverse may be used particularly to demonstrate what the site of the town was like, and the stages of development of the growing spread of buildings. This involves a start at the historic core, and a series of walks along fairly straight lines through the contrasting zones which demonstrate the outward urban growth. For each walk, a base map in the form of a long strip on a scale of 25 or 50 inches to a mile is prepared, covering a narrow strip, a street or two wide, and extending from the town centre to a point in the outer suburbs. On this strip, all significant features are recorded, such as changes in the general slope of the land, in the building pattern, or in the ages or functions of buildings, observable zonal boundaries, and buildings of historical and architectural interest.

After the completion of the field work, a transect diagram is built up. At the foot of the page, draw a line to represent the rise and fall of the ground, but without too much exaggeration of vertical scale. Draw a series of vertical lines from points where the slope changes. This will form a series of columns, each one attached to one part of the cross-section. It may well be found that a particular type of building, terraced working-class houses, predominates in a given area; this can be drawn in the relevant column, and labelled appropriately.

A series of horizontal lines drawn across the space above the section intersects the vertical lines and divides the space into box-like compartments. Each horizontal zone is assigned a heading, such as Gradient of Roads, Industries and Workshops, Type of Housing, Age of Buildings, Type of Transport, Availability of Shopping Facilities, and so on. As each compartment is related vertically to the recognizable urban sub-division below, and horizontally to the heading, the completed transect table presents a large body of information in summary form. The transect table is the geographer's most convenient way of recording the principal changes along a strip running from the centre of the town as far as the outskirts.

A GENERALIZED LAND USE MAP OF A TOWN

As a sequel to the completion of a series of urban transects, the information may be combined in a number of comprehensive maps of the town as a whole.

The key map is one showing land use, in a fairly generalized way, as shown from the map of Gloucester in Fig. 34.

A FUNCTIONAL ZONE MAP

The map of Gloucester (Fig. 35) is a further generalization from the facts shown in the land use map.

A GROWTH MAP

The functional regions map is in turn closely related to one showing the stages by which the town has grown to its present extent (Fig. 36).This map should be based, so far as possible, on observation of dates and styles of building, but additional help may be obtained from old maps. For most county towns, street maps drawn by John Speed in 1610 provide valuable information about the earliest stages of the growth of the core.

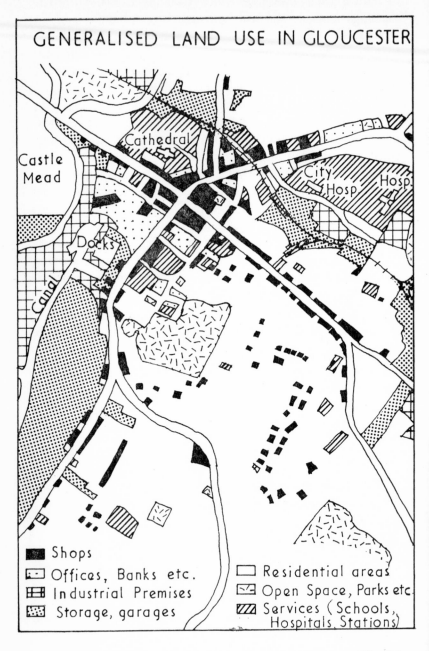

GENERALISED LAND USE IN GLOUCESTER

Castle
Mead

Cathedral

City
Hosp

Hosp

Docks

Canal

Shops
Offices, Banks etc.
Industrial Premises
Storage, garages

Residential areas
Open Space, Parks etc.
Services (Schools,
Hospitals, Stations)

Fig. 34

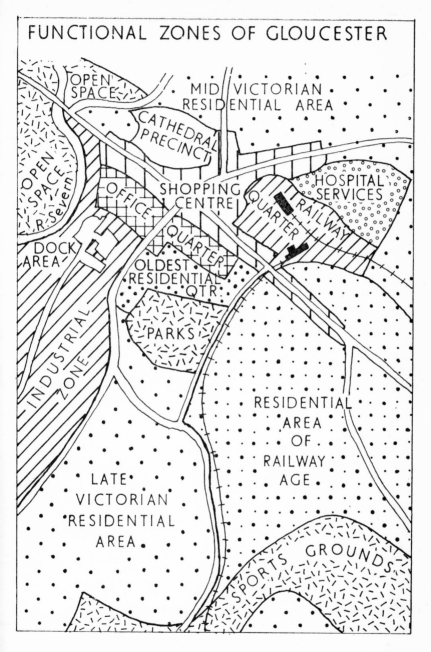

FUNCTIONAL ZONES OF GLOUCESTER

OPEN SPACE

MID VICTORIAN RESIDENTIAL AREA

CATHEDRAL PRECINCT

OPEN SPACE R. Severn

OFFICE QUARTER

SHOPPING CENTRE

RAILWAY QUARTER

HOSPITAL SERVICES

RAILWAY

DOCK AREA

OLDEST RESIDENTIAL QTR.

PARKS

INDUSTRIAL ZONE

RESIDENTIAL AREA OF RAILWAY AGE

LATE VICTORIAN RESIDENTIAL AREA

SPORTS GROUNDS

Fig. 35

91

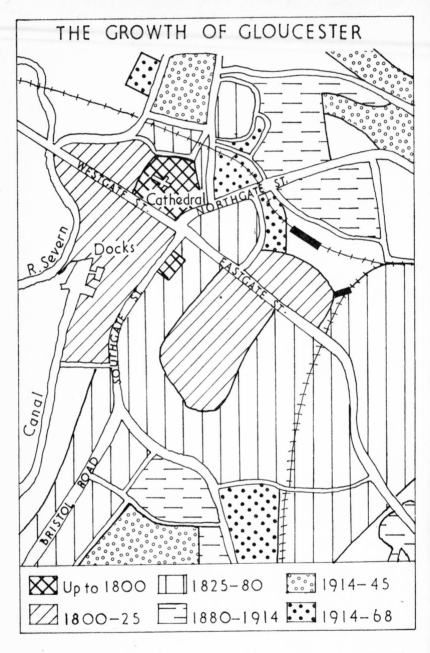

THE GROWTH OF GLOUCESTER

R. Severn
WESTGATE ST.
Cathedral
NORTHGATE ST.
Docks
EASTGATE ST.
SOUTHGATE ST.
Canal
BRISTOL ROAD

⊠ Up to 1800	▥ 1825–80	⊙ 1914–45
▧ 1800–25	▤ 1880–1914	⦂ 1914–68

Fig. 36

More generally available are the successive editions of Ordnance Survey maps from 1801 up to the present day. Additional assistance for drawing an urban growth map may be obtained from old directories.

Long-established towns often reveal one or other of a number of distinctive spatial structures. The commonest of these is the concentric sequence of roughly circular zones, in the following order:

1. The Central Business District of public buildings, office blocks, large stores and specialized shops, with few if any dwellings (page 59).

2. The Inner Zone or Twilight Zone upon which 'urban blight' has visibly laid its hand in the form of obsolete buildings and buildings which have changed their function. In places, redevelopment and replacement is taking place, often marked by the construction of blocks of flats and the replanning of streets to create inner ring roads.

3. A discontinuous belt of heavy industry, often associated with a group of river or canal wharves or with goods stations or sidings, and located at what was in Victorian times the edge of the town.

4. A residential zone of Victorian or Edwardian terraced housing, with monotonous rows of houses with a uniform roofline, dramatically broken at intervals by the sudden uprise of tall Church spires, multi-storeyed factories and Board schools or hospitals.

5. A more spacious and open-textured residential zone of semi-detached villas and municipal housing built between the two World Wars. There are many tree-shaded avenues, and a generous provision of parks and open spaces. There are occasional factory estates and shopping centres.

6. Very recent suburbs, often containing tall slabby blocks of flats.

7. A series of clusters (rather than a continuous zone) of upper-class commuters' residences just outside the urban fringe, but convenient to stations or main roads which assist rapid daily travel towards the town's centre.

THE IMPACT OF RECENT IDEAS ON TOWN PLANNING

New forms of town-layout have evolved to meet the needs of the 1960's, with a view to the expectations of the 1970's. It is likely that one or other of these concepts of town-planning has influenced the arrangement of buildings, streets and open spaces in the most modern sections of the town.

THE NEIGHBOURHOOD UNIT

The theory behind the concept of the neighbourhood is that, in order to foster the life of a community, it is necessary to break down the totality of a town's population into groups which are small enough to acquire a sense of identification with a locality. What is important is that a town should be broken down for many purposes into a series of, as it were, inward-looking villages within the area of the town. Only for special purposes, such as work or entertainment, should the inhabitants of a neighbourhood unit need to go outside their locality. It should have its own group of shops catering for the essential requirements of life, its social centre (the Neighbourhood Centre), its own secondary school and a number of tributary primary schools, its own clinic, banks and post office, and recreational space of its own.

The Neighbourhood Unit is the area of a community of people, small enough to acquire a sense of local identification, but large enough to support a secondary school. This requires at least 5000 people. The pattern of the neighbourhood is determined by convenience of access from home to school and community centre, and by the policy of making major traffic routes go round it and not through it.

Many of the post-war New Towns around London, such as Crawley New Town and Stevenage, were planned as a series of neighbourhood units. The major road system and belts of open space divided the neighbourhoods from one another. Certain areas were set aside for industry and open space. All the neighbourhoods converged upon the town centre, which contained more elaborate facilities than the neighbourhood centres.

The only objections to the neighbourhood principle, as it was applied in the New Towns of the 1950's, were that they took up so much space that they were costly to live in, and that people were so wedded to separate family living that any sense of community was difficult to build up. It was possible to speak of 'new town blues', the sense of isolation which arises when the bright lights of the town centre are so distant that the effort involved in travelling centrewards is too great, and people therefore prefer to sit at home in front of their television sets.

A later stage in the evolution of the neighbourhood principle has been the attempt to provide an environment for social groups rather than for single families. This was a reaction against the individualism which had tended to run riot. The appropriate type of building for the social group was the tall slab-block of family flats. This was economical of space and building costs, since the slab-block is the shape that gives the greatest floor space in relation to space for circulation or movement. There was every likelihood of building up the spirit of group-living when the flats were let to families who hitherto had lived in the congested streets of obsolete houses which this new housing was designed to replace. There was, it was felt, a sense of security engendered by being surrounded by already familiar faces, and a degree of kinship from having shared the same experiences before coming to live in the slab-block.

THE HIGH DENSITY TOWN

The break from the Neighbourhood Unit principle came about 1960 with the planning of the new town of Cumbernauld, between Stirling and Glasgow. The first stage in the building of this town was opened in 1967. Cumbernauld has been planned as one centralized town for 70,000 people on a hilltop site, two miles long and one mile wide. It is compactly designed as a high density town, with about 90 people to every acre living in ranges of houses, all with private open spaces attached to them (Fig. 37).

The town is surrounded by ring roads, but the vehicular approach to the town centre is circuitous. Pedestrians, however, enjoy a complete network of pedestrian ways leading directly to the multi-level town centre from which no one will be far distant. Parts of these pedestrian ways are leafy lanes, other parts are flights of shallow steps and flagged paths among the houses,

9

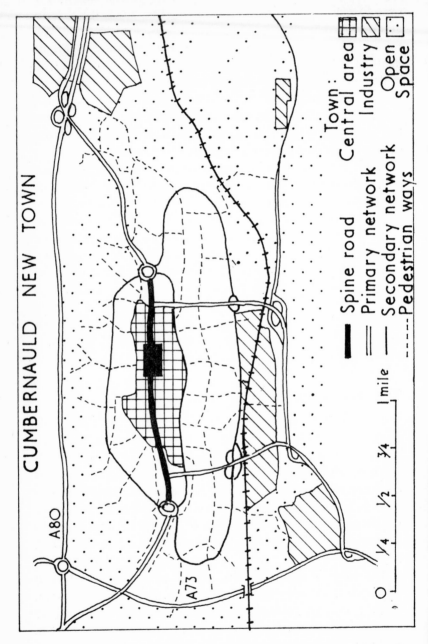

CUMBERNAULD NEW TOWN

Town:
Central area
Industry
Open Space

Spine road
Primary network
Secondary network
Pedestrian ways

A80

A73

0 ¼ ½ ¾ 1 mile

Fig. 37

giving variety and interest to the short walk to the city centre. Although Cumbernauld is planned on the principle that most families have a car, it is also planned on the assumption that they will leave their cars at home when they make their way on foot to the town centre.

The town centre is a monolithic block divided into many levels. Pedestrians hold sway at ground level, cars are parked at first floor level and above this are shops, a church, a cinema and to crown all a roof-top open space to serve as viewpoint and restful garden. Escalators give access to the upper levels. Already Cumbernauld is proving to be a town of character, though there is some criticism of the closeness with which houses are packed together.

Cumbernauld's road system is an example of the Radburn type of layout, named after its American designer (Fig. 38).

THE SERIAL VISION TOWN

A new conception of town planning is gaining vogue, which seeks to combine the good qualities of the neighbourhood unit town, the high density town, together with the new or reborn idea of a town which shall appear as a linked sequence of masses and spaces. This calls for a town where there are quiet, enclosed spaces separate from, but linked to, spaces full of hustling and bustling activity. The whole town will enfold itself to the visitor as a sequence of contrasted spaces, which arouse curiosity about what new there will be to see on passing through the archway to the next space, until he reaches the space in the very heart of the town which forms a climax to the whole. The whole concept is known to architects as serial vision of a town which appeals, not by reason of the individual buildings that make it up, but because of the qualities of the solid masses and the void spaces which are linked together to make up the town as a whole.

Work is progressing on a new town to be sited on marshland close to Woolwich in South-East London. It is called Thamesmead. Figs. 39 and 40 show the main features of the projected layout.

Why is this site likely to be important industrially?

What unusual features are planned for the town centre?

THE PRINCIPLE OF
RADBURN PLANNING

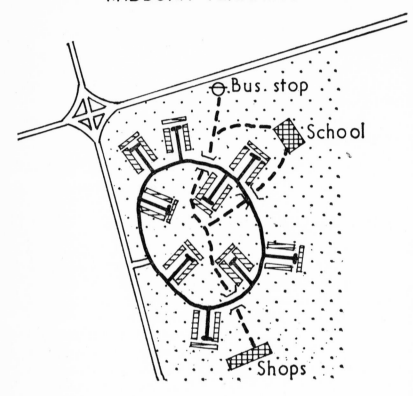

Bus. stop

School

Shops

═══ Distributor roads

▬▬ Access roads

− − − Pedestrian ways

▤ Housing

⠒⠒ Areas of pedestrian freedom

Fig. 38

What is notable about the distribution of open space in and around Thamesmead?

What part will the River Thames, lakes and canals play in the layout of the town?

In what ways does the pattern of through roads differ from that of access roads, and in turn from the pattern of pedestrian ways?

Do you regard the circulation of vehicles and pedestrians to have been planned to the best advantage?

Summarize the unusual features which form part of the planning of Thamesmead.

THE DISPERSED CITY

Many town planners believe that the greatest problem of our times is how to adapt our present towns, and to build new towns, fully to meet the needs of an age of increasing family car ownership.

This conclusion stems from three facts: the growing number of one (or even two) car-owning families, the decreasing size of families, and the increasing number of car trips which people take outside working hours. The present number of cars in Great Britain is about 10 millions: this will probably double by 1980 A.D. and quadruple by 2000 A.D. At the same time, the average family which comprised four people in 1920 now consists of three people, and will be less than $2\frac{1}{2}$ on average by 1980. There is, in addition a marked trend towards an increasing number of car journeys: whereas from 1962 to 1981 it is estimated that work-journeys in London by bus or train will rise by a mere 10 per cent, business trips by car will increase by 105 per cent, shopping trips by 90 per cent, journeys to school by 123 per cent and social journeys by 74 per cent. At this rate, the projected new road to cross London from east to west will need to be a 14–lane highway.

The town of the future can hardly be thought of in terms of a congested core providing jobs and major shopping facilities for open-textured residential suburbs from which most people commute daily. The centrally-orientated town must give place to the open patterned city, consisting of many nuclei linked by broad highways which can cope with the diffuse cross-hauling which the future will bring, and amply provided with parking space.

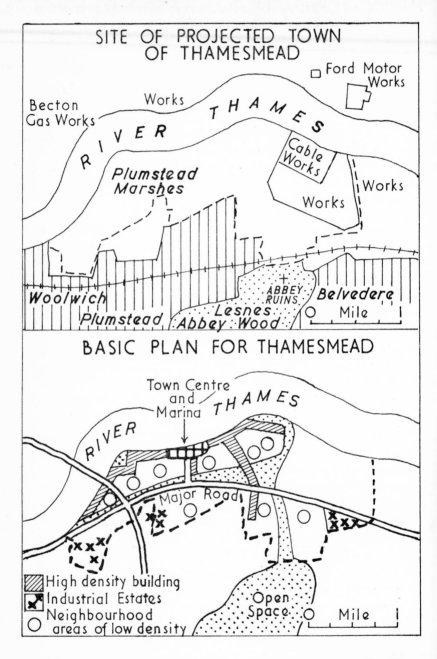

SITE OF PROJECTED TOWN OF THAMESMEAD

Ford Motor Works

Becton Gas Works

Works

RIVER THAMES

Plumstead Marshes

Cable Works

Works

Works

Woolwich

Plumstead

Lesnes Abbey Wood

ABBEY RUINS

Belvedere

Mile

BASIC PLAN FOR THAMESMEAD

Town Centre and Marina

RIVER THAMES

Major Road

High density building
Industrial Estates
Neighbourhood areas of low density

Open Space

Mile

Fig. 39

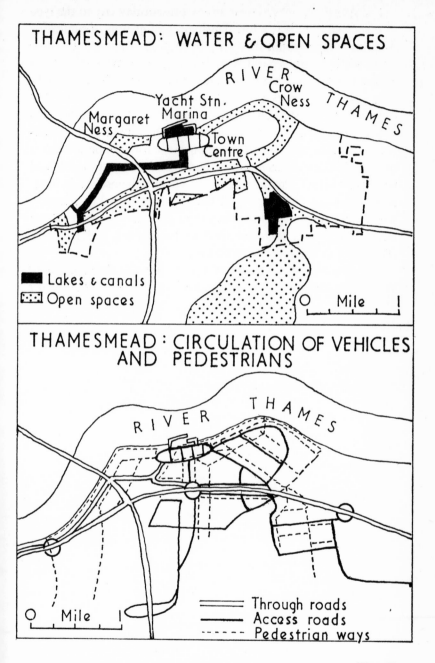

THAMESMEAD: WATER & OPEN SPACES

RIVER THAMES

Crow Ness

Yacht Stn.
Marina

Margaret
Ness

Town
Centre

■ Lakes & canals
▓ Open spaces

0   Mile   1

THAMESMEAD: CIRCULATION OF VEHICLES
AND PEDESTRIANS

RIVER THAMES

0   Mile   1

══ Through roads
── Access roads
--- Pedestrian ways

Fig. 40

101

Los Angeles comes as near as any present-day city to the type of dispersed city. It is a low density city of groups of bungalow dwellings, each within its own plot of grass and shrubs. These small sections are separated by broad motorways and parking spaces so extensive that the two make up two-thirds of the available space. Shoppers journey, not inwards to the centre, but outwards to the shopping parades and huge supermarkets provided with vast parking spaces built on the outskirts. This subtracts from the town centre the importance for shopping which it once had. Drive-in restaurants, banks and the motels designed to house visitors' cars as well as the visitors themselves in overnight stays are multiplying on the approaches to Los Angeles, where land is so much less costly than near the city centre. New office blocks and factories tend to be erected, not near the centre, but in the outermost suburbs.

Los Angeles poses the questions: Is the city disintegrating? Will urban life as we have come to know it eventually disappear?

CALCULATING AN AMENITY INDEX FOR YOUR HOME

Is your home well placed in respect of amenities, or do you find it slow and difficult to reach other places from it?

Is your home better placed than your friend's home in another part of the town?

Both of you may try to settle the argument by working out the amenity index for his own home.

The index may be worked out by counting the number of paces from home to each of the main amenities.

Here is an example.

Amenity	Number of paces from home
1. Bus stop	250
2. Railway station	Beyond walking distance
3. Primary school	915
4. Provision shop	821
5. Butcher's shop	803
6. Draper's shop	1613
7. Newsagent's shop	805
8. Park or playing field	892
9. Chemist's shop	1689
10. Telephone box	27

Add an estimate of each place which is beyond walking distance.

Estimated distance to Railway station	3000
Total	10,815

Divide by 10, as this is the total number of amenities, giving 1081.5 as the amenity index for the house in the example. A low index means that the home is in a well-serviced suburb. A high index indicates a home remote from amenities, situated in the heart of 'a desert of housing'.

OLD FIELDS AND MODERN STREET LAYOUT IN NOTTINGHAM

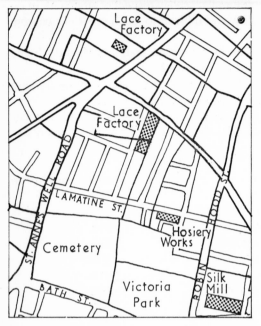

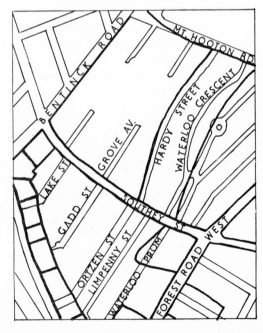

Fig. 41

104

5

THE TOWN AS A PLACE FOR MOVEMENT

THE MANY PURPOSES OF STREETS

The reason why streets are often so congested is they have to serve so many different purposes at one and the same time. In the past, many streets in the centres of towns could serve all needs and habits. For example, Regent Street in London was laid out in the form of a sweeping curve by the architect John Nash between the years 1813 and 20. It was designed as an artery for traffic through the heart of the West End, extending from Regent's Park to the Mall and Buckingham Palace, along which the Prince Regent (later King George IV) might drive in comfort and state. Beneath the road, the main north-south sewer was hidden, to convey the sewage of North London into the Thames. Regent Street was also a public parade, where the well-dressed and the flashily dressed might see and be seen underneath the rows of columns or colonnades flanking the street. It was also a shopping centre, drawing its labour from Soho to its east side and its clients from Mayfair to the west. The street served also as a boundary between the rich of Mayfair and the poor of Soho. Thus, Regent Street was multiple in its functions. Today, its functions have been added to, as underground railways, gas and electricity mains run beneath it. The costs of maintaining shops in the street are so high that the colonnades have been removed and the buildings heightened to provide more shopping space, but to the detriment of the appearance of the street. So great is the traffic that the whole road is often snarled up with buses, taxis, lorries and private cars, and is in danger of losing the beauty and style which it once had.

THE MULTI-PURPOSE STREET

It is an easy task to go to any street in any town and make a complete list of its functions, and to judge if any of these functions is tending to dominate and drive into the background all the others. It will need a little detective work to ascertain what is the purpose of the manholes and valve covers in the street, but usually they bear initial letters which show to what service they belong. It is a good idea to plot the position, say, of all the air valves on a large scale plan of the street, and from the evidence to plot the course of the sewer, the gas or electricity main or the underground telephone cable. A watch on holes in the road when these are dug to attend to buried pipes and cables will give much help in tracing these courses.

THE STREET AS A RELIC OF THE PAST

The street pattern of the present is often directly derived from the field pattern of the past. It is instructive to put side by side a present-day street map and a Tithe Map of the period 1830–40 or an earlier Estate Map and note the ways in which the twists and curves in modern streets reflect the irregularities in the boundaries of the fields which they replaced.

What decided where residential streets should be placed? They were often laid out by speculative builders, and to build they needed land. Builders bought up fields one by one whenever farmers were tempted to sell. Into these they had to fit buildings and streets. The latter were linked with the winding tracks along which farmers had driven their carts to collect their crops of hay or wheat. If a pre-existing field had a sharp angle at one corner, a brow-shaped house, shaped to fit into an acute angle at the corner of a field, often perpetuates its shape. Fig. 41 shows the legacy of old field shapes to the modern street layout in two contrasted parts of Nottingham.

THE STREET AS A USER OF SPACE

Roads inevitably occupy a substantial part of the available space. The proportion of space varies greatly from town to town. In a densely built-up mining town of South Wales, laid out in a period when it was believed that railways and canals would serve to move goods and people, the roads, garages and car-parks may occupy a mere 20 per cent of the built-up area. In the 'dispersed city' of Los Angeles, in which the needs of private motorcar transport dominate the plan, with ample provision of fast highways and ample parking spaces attached to factories, shops, banks, offices and churches, the proportion rises to 70 per cent (page 102).

Select a number of contrasting areas from your town. Trace from a map on squared paper a portion of each, making all the portions of each sample of the same size, and count the number of squares which are covered by roads or car parks. Calculate the percentage of each sample which is given over to the needs of traffic. Compare the figures obtained for the various areas.

TREES IN A STREET

One function of a residential street is for people to stand and talk. To this end, the shade of trees and the changing seasonal colours of foliage, is a help. One of the most celebrated and pleasing streets in the world is the Lijnbaan in Rotterdam, a traffic-free precinct with a lime tree at its centre. There are plenty of seats for shoppers to rest in, and a paved space on which, in the spring, flower heads are laid out to form floral pictures.

Too often we fail to realize the extent to which shady and colourful trees contribute to the visual appearance of our streets. On a sketch map of a group of streets, map the position of all trees in or near a street, so as to appreciate the pattern of planting. Distinguish between fully mature trees and recently planted ones. A small circle may be drawn round the dot to show the extent of the space shaded by its outstretched branches (Fig. 42).

Which gives the best effect – trees on one side of the road only (Seabrooke Road in Fig. 42), on both sides closely spaced (Malvern Road) or widely spaced (North Road) or in a clump (Girls' High School Grounds)?

Assess the relative advantages and disadvantages of tree planting on roads. (Among the latter are the inconveniences of autumn leaf-fall, and drip from wet leaves.)

NOISE IN STREETS

Much thought is now being given to methods of spacing buildings in relationship to roads in such a way as to reduce as far as possible the noise and vibration which accompany the movement of heavy traffic.

TREES IN AN URBAN AREA :
RESIDENTIAL STREETS IN GLOUCESTER

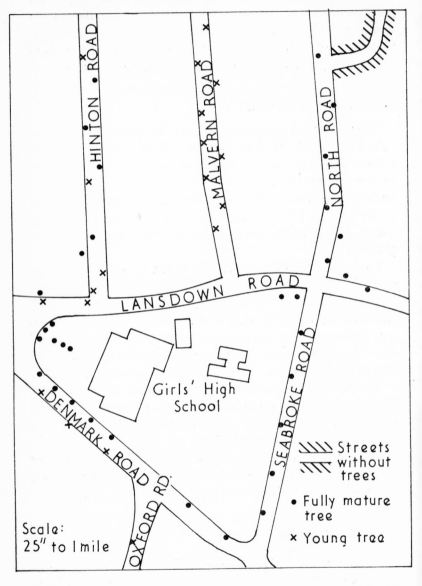

Streets without trees

• Fully mature tree

× Young tree

Scale: 25" to 1 mile

Girls' High School

Fig. 42

Fig. 43 shows three methods which have been suggested for combating noise in towns. In each case, the dotted lines represent the waves of sound issuing from the passing vehicles on a three-line highway, and a suggested method of arranging the residential buildings in relationship to the road. In the first of the three methods, empty space acts as noise barrier between road and residences, but in the third a factory building serves this purpose. In the second, the residences adjoin the road.

> Which method is likely, in your opinion, to be the most effective noise-combating method of the three?
> Which is the most economical, and which the least economical, of space?
> Which method is best designed to serve the needs of those wishing to cross the highway from time to time?
> Which method adds to the appearance of the district and which detracts from it?

THE STREET AS A DUMPING GROUND

While some seek to beautify our streets with trees and flower-beds, others find it necessary to make of it a general dumping ground, particularly on refuse collection days. Dustbins, milk bottles, parking space for garageless cars and motorcycles, and car washing must compete for space with the other users of the road, and must seriously detract from its appearance.

> Mark on a sketch-map of a small group of streets the unsightly excrescences, such as all-night parked vehicles, dustbins on collecting days, and evidence of car washing in the street.
> What measures would you suggest to improve the tidiness and orderliness of these streets?

TRAFFIC IN STREETS

Traffic is the blood stream of the urban organism. Once the circulatory flow between the heart and the ends of the limbs becomes sluggish or clotted, paralysis of the whole body begins. Traffic surveys are necessary to measure the state of health of the town's circulatory system.

COMBATING TRAFFIC NOISE IN TOWNS

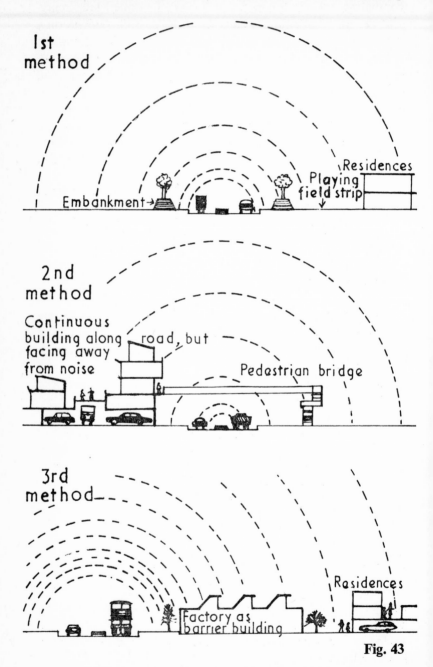

1st method

Embankment→ Residences

Playing field strip

2nd method

Continuous building along road, but facing away from noise

Pedestrian bridge

3rd method

Residences

Factory as barrier building

Fig. 43

A Traffic Census may be conducted at any convenient point on a road, railway, canal or navigable river. For a road survey, a page in a notebook should be ruled into five columns. One is headed 'Cycles and motorcycles', the second 'Lorries', the third 'Buses and other forms of Public Transport', the fourth 'Motor Cars and Light Vehicles' and the last 'Heavy Vehicles' (with six wheels or weighing over 30 cwt.).

A position is taken up overlooking the road, preferably from a window. As each vehicle passes, a mark is speedily placed in the appropriate column. If there are two observers, each may record the traffic going in one direction. The record may be made for a number of short periods during the day, so as to get an average value of the day's traffic. More significantly, the census may be taken for a number of differing times, such as the morning rush hour, the lunch-time reduction in flow almost to a lull, and finally the period of the evening return from work.

It is possible to calculate whether the road is officially over-crowded or not, according to Ministry of Transport standards, by working out the average volume of traffic per hour, measured in Passenger Car Units (P.C.Us.). This is done by allowing $\frac{1}{2}$ P.C.U. for every cycle or motorcycle counted within the space of one hour, 1 P.C.U. for every motorcar or light vehicle, 2 P.C.Us. for every lorry or bus, and 3 P.C.Us. for every heavy vehicle. The total number of Passenger Car Units per hour can be obtained by addition. A circle may be drawn to represent this total, and the circle subdivided, either to show the shares attributable to the different forms of transport, or, as has been done in Fig 44, to show the proportions attached to the different roads which converge upon the census point.

The official maximum figures are as follows. When these are exceeded, the road is regarded as overcrowded.

375 P.C.Us. is the limit for a 24 ft. 2-lane carriageway.
688 P.C.Us. is the limit for a 33 ft. 3-lane carriageway.
1512 P.C.Us. is the limit for a 48 ft. dual 2-lane carriage-way.

A large plan of the crossroads may be drawn and the survey shown graphically by coloured arrows of proportionate width.

MAKING A TRAFFIC CENSUS

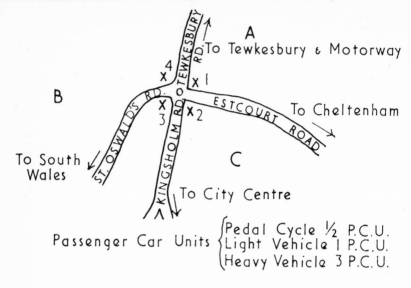

A. To Tewkesbury & Motorway

To Cheltenham

To South Wales

To City Centre

Passenger Car Units $\begin{cases} \text{Pedal Cycle } \frac{1}{2} \text{ P.C.U.} \\ \text{Light Vehicle } 1 \text{ P.C.U.} \\ \text{Heavy Vehicle } 3 \text{ P.C.U.} \end{cases}$

TRAFFIC DENSITY IN ONE HOUR

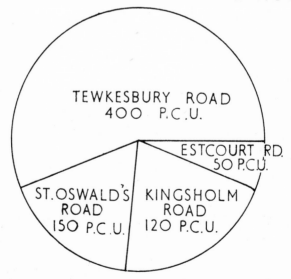

TEWKESBURY ROAD
400 P.C.U.

ESTCOURT RD.
50 P.C.U.

ST. OSWALD'S ROAD
150 P.C.U.

KINGSHOLM ROAD
120 P.C.U.

Fig. 44

A THROUGH AND STOPPING TRAFFIC SURVEY

This type of survey is designed to show which are the busiest approaches to a group of streets, such as a shopping centre, and also the proportion of through and stopping traffic. Two small groups of enumerators are placed on each of the approaches to the centre, provided with watches and ruled scored sheet. One group checks incoming traffic and the other the outgoing traffic. Before leaving for the recording points, watches should be carefully synchronized.

At zero hour, the first member of each group of enumerators calls out the time every half minute and the second calls out the last three digits of the numbers of passing cars, while the third records both types of information on the score sheet. After the survey period is over, all groups assemble and compare their figures to ascertain which are the busiest roads. They also find the grand total of the incoming and the outgoing vehicles. There will be a difference between the totals; this gives an indication of the number of vehicles stopping within the area.

A more precise result may be obtained by making a list of the incoming car numbers, and asking those who have the numbers of the outgoing cars which numbers are missing from their lists.

It is also possible from the figures to measure the time which each vehicle spent in passing through the area, by subtracting the time of its incoming to the time of its outgoing. Some cars, of course, will have no exit time. Others will have spent a period of time in the area, having parked for a time to make a shopping or other form of visit. Others will have passed through without stopping, but with considerable delay owing to traffic congestion, while others will have passed through at some other time without delay. This analysis gives a variety of figures, which, when expressed in diagrammatic form, will give a graphic picture of the behaviour of traffic within the area studied.

THE TIME AND COST OF THE JOURNEY TO WORK

It is instructive to pool information from a family group about the time and money which the various members spend in travelling to and from work. Fig. 45 shows how this has been done for the members of a single family. It also shows by means of a histogram the range of amounts paid out by all the families represented in a school class.

A JOURNEY–TO-WORK COST SURVEY

Table for one family:

Worker	Daily cost	Work days per week	Weekly Total
Father (car)	1s. 3d petrol 6d parking	6	10s. 6d.
Sister (bus)	10d. fare	5	4s. 2d.
Brother (motorcycle)	10d. petrol	6	5s. 0d.
		Total	19s. 8d.
		Average per person	6s 7d

HISTOGRAM OF AVERAGE WEEKLY COST OF JOURNEY-TO-WORK OF FAMILIES REPRESENTED IN A CLASS

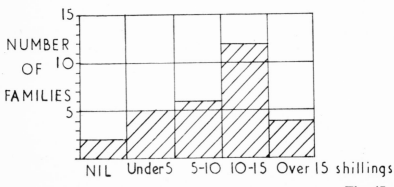

Fig. 45

6

THE TOWN AS A CENTRE OF
A WIDER AREA

A town cannot live in isolation; it both supports and is supported by the countryside by which it is surrounded. Many of our towns grew up in the past as market centres for an agricultural neighbourhood. In exchange for their food, the people of the countryside came to expect the specialized services of the town's craftsmen and merchants. At first market towns were closely spaced, because the limit to which a farmer could be expected to drive his cattle or carry his wheat to the market, and to walk home again after transacting his business, was about three miles. This meant that market towns were only about six miles apart.

In the last century or two, men have become much more mobile, but are still reluctant to travel to work or market for more than an hour by bus, car or train, just as were their ancestors who walked to town. The area within which people tend to look to one town is often called the urban field, on the analogy of the magnetic field within which particles of iron filings are attracted to the pole of a bar magnet. Sometimes it is referred to as a zone of urban influence, or urban hinterland, or a word of German origin, 'umland' or 'round-about-land' is used.

There are certain limits to the area within which the urban-rural link is practicable, usually set at about an hour's journey from the town, but less or more than this at any particular point in response to a variety of factors. The discovery of the extent of an urban field is a matter of great practical importance for commerce and industry. Any manufacturer whose products are in wide demand must decide for himself the centres from which he will distribute his goods, and the *umland* which each depot must serve. If this manufacturer uses local raw material, whether it be gravel for making concrete, milk for making ice-cream or barley for brewing beer, he must decide his processing centres and the *umland* from which each will draw. The smaller manufacturer who relies upon public transport for distribution of his wares, especially if these are perishable or must be regularly and

115

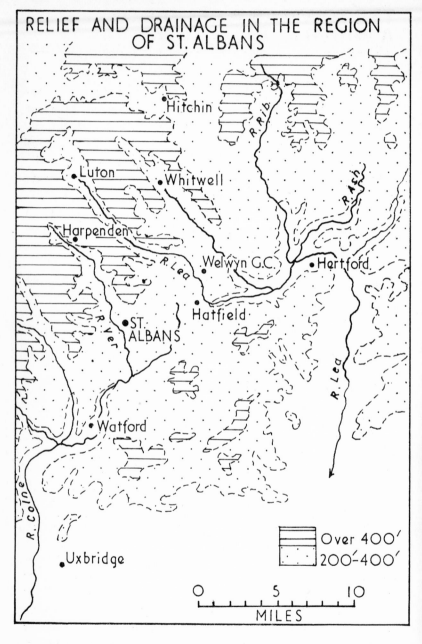

RELIEF AND DRAINAGE IN THE REGION OF ST. ALBANS

Over 400'
200'–400'

MILES

Fig. 46

promptly delivered, is very much concerned with the extent of the urban field.

METHODS OF SHOWING THE URBAN FIELDS OF SMALLER TOWNS

The best of the methods devised to set limits to the urban field of a smaller town is by plotting the frequency of local bus services into it. There is a point between two towns which acts as a sort of human watershed; on one side people tend to move to Town A and the other to Town B. This is reflected in the frequency of bus services into these towns, particularly on market days when the town really comes into its own as the meeting place of the rural community which it sustains (Fig. 46). A local bus time-table will list the number of buses per day using the roads feeding the town, and when the roads are traced from a small-scale map, and thickened in proportion to the number of buses per day which pass along them in either direction, the result is a flow line diagram which is very revealing (Fig. 47).

Is the pattern of flow towards St. Albans relatively even from all sides, or are there certain preferred directions of flow?

The area to the east of St. Albans is largely the lowland of the Lea Valley, with relatively few settlements, while to the north-west lies the mid-Hertfordshire Plateau, with many industrial and residential settlements.

How is this fact reflected in the bus-transport pattern?

Harpenden and Hatfield have not such large shopping centres as St. Albans.

How is this reflected in the bus-flow pattern?

Harpenden has many factories which are subsidiaries of larger concerns in St. Albans.

How does this affect the pattern?

Much valuable data is missed if the flow diagram merely covers bus services in general, as a measure of accessibility to the town. Buses run at various hours of the day and on different days of the week. Thus, early morning bus services designed particularly for factory workers, rather than for office and shop

117

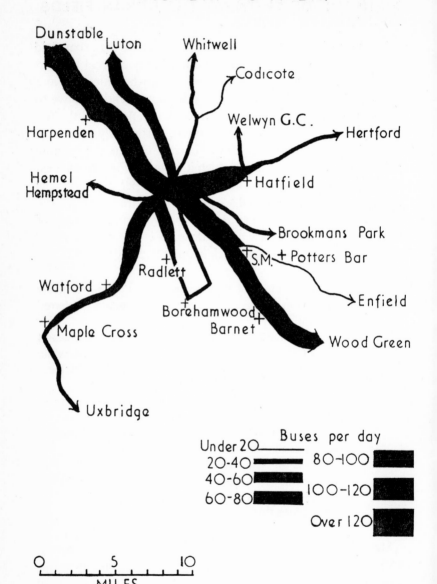

BUS-FLOW LINES FROM ST. ALBANS
MONDAY TO FRIDAY

Dunstable

Luton

Whitwell

Codicote

Harpenden

Welwyn G.C.

Hertford

Hemel Hempstead

Hatfield

Brookmans Park

Radlett

S.M.

Potters Bar

Watford

Enfield

Borehamwood

Maple Cross

Barnet

Wood Green

Uxbridge

Buses per day

Under 20

20-40

40-60

60-80

80-100

100-120

Over 120

0   5   10

MILES

Fig. 47a

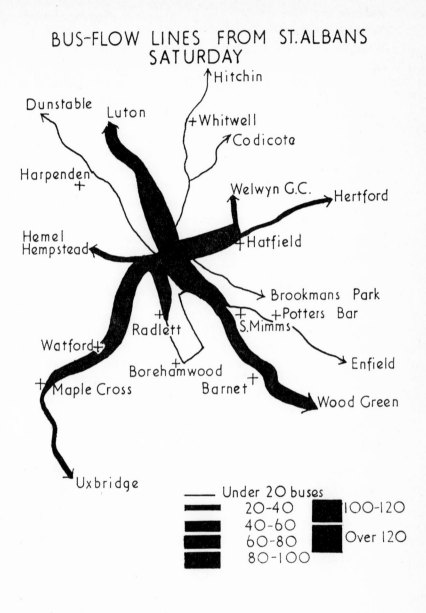

BUS-FLOW LINES FROM ST.ALBANS
SATURDAY

↑Hitchin

Dunstable

Luton

+Whitwell

↗Codicote

Harpenden +

Welwyn G.C. → Hertford

Hemel
Hempstead ←

+Hatfield

↘ Brookmans Park

+Potters Bar

S.Mimms +

Radlett +

Watford +

↘ Enfield

Borehamwood +

Maple Cross +

Barnet +

→ Wood Green

↙Uxbridge

_____ Under 20 buses

20-40

▮▮▮ 100-120

40-60

60-80

▮ Over 120

80-100

0   5   10

MILES

Fig. 47b

119

workers, may give valuable clues to the areas from which local factories draw their employees—information otherwise not available except when, through the kindness of factory managers, they are willing to list the areas from which they draw their labour force. Buses running at mid-morning and mid-afternoon are mainly designed for shoppers. Late buses, leaving at 9 p.m. or later, give some indication of the localities whose residents can take advantage of entertainments, late-night restaurants and evening functions in town. Market day buses, as has already been pointed out, indicate the extent of the area from which buyers and sellers in the market are regularly drawn (Fig. 47). Sunday buses may give some idea of the area within which social journeys to the town to visit relations and friends are made. Special hospital bus services, too, are an indication of the area from which patients and their visitors are drawn.

SATURDAY IS ST. ALBANS' MARKET DAY

Is the bus flow heavier or lighter in general on Saturdays?
On what routes is the bus traffic lighter on Saturdays?
On what routes is the bus traffic heavier on Saturdays?
Whipsnade Zoo is near Dunstable. Is it more desirable to plan a trip to it from St. Albans on a Saturday or on another day of the week? Give a reason.

ISOCHRONE MAP

An isochrone map demonstrates the distance from the town centre which can be reached within a given time by a certain mode of transport. Isochrones are lines drawn to link all places which lie at, say, five, ten or fifteen miles travelling time from the centre, and may easily be drawn from the information provided by a time-table, supplemented by personal experience (Figs. 48 and 49).

From St. Albans, the ground rises to the west and descends to the east.
How is this reflected in the shape of the bus isochrones?
The road from the bus garage to the City Station has very heavy traffic.

How is this reflected in the shape of the bus isochrone for five minutes?

Beyond the City Station there are few compulsory
stops or traffic lights.

How does this affect the isochrones?

THE CIRCULATION AREA OF A WEEKLY NEWSPAPER

Special importance may be claimed for the circulation area of a weekly newspaper as an indicator of the field of an urban centre. This newspaper, published and distributed over the surrounding district, contains advertisements which lose their point if they are not read by persons who may respond to them by desiring to purchase the goods advertised, whether they be houses or lollipops. Hence, if all the places mentioned in the advertisements in an issue of the paper are marked by dots on a map, and a line drawn to enclose the main concentration of dots, we have an indication of the extent of the area within which that week's advertisers have, from experience, deemed it likely to secure customers for their wares (Fig. 50).

The weekly newspaper also reflects the existence of social associations in the neighbourhood of the town. Reports of society and club activities, whether social, religious, musical or sporting, largely make up the contents of such newspapers, to-gether with reports of the proceedings of local Councils and the police courts. However, besides reflecting the existence of social organizations, a local newspaper can serve as a focus for fostering a sense of community based upon neighbourhood. If, through the pages of the newspaper, its editor or some local leader runs a campaign to curb danger to children at a particularly dangerous road crossing, a feeling of common indignation and zeal for improvement may sweep through the entire readership of the paper and serve to link them in a common cause. This feeling of community may last, long after the campaign for betterment is over, particularly if it has been successful in its aim.

The *Hertfordshire Advertiser* is published in St. Albans.
Other newspapers are published in Luton, Watford and
Hemel Hempstead.

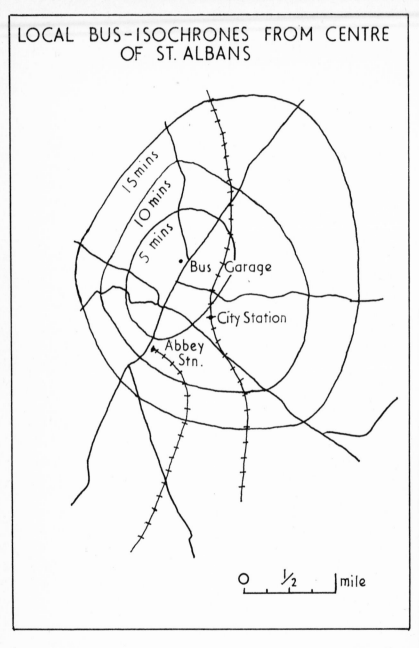

LOCAL BUS-ISOCHRONES FROM CENTRE OF ST. ALBANS

15 mins

10 mins

5 mins

Bus Garage

City Station

Abbey Stn.

O ½ mile

Fig. 48

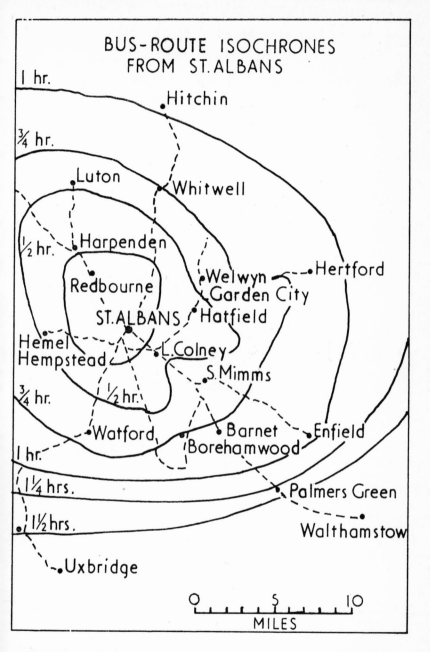

Fig. 49

CIRCULATION AREA OF
"THE HERTFORDSHIRE ADVERTISER"
Based on reports of news items and on
mentions in advertisements.

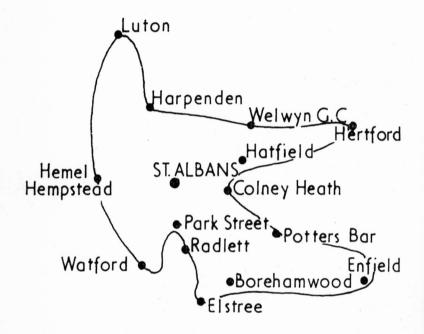

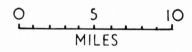

MILES

Fig. 50

How are the facts reflected in the circulation area of the first-named paper?

Hertford is the County Town, and many events of county importance take place there, and many jobs in county administrative offices are available.

How does this affect the circulations area of the St. Albans' paper?

Luton is the largest industrial centre, and so commands much advertising space.

How is this reflected in the shape of the circulation area?

THE CIRCULATION AREA OF A PROVINCIAL DAILY

Larger towns have the publication of an evening or even a morning newspaper as part of their urban equipment. The circulation area of a provincial daily newspaper is of exceptional importance as reflecting the city's effective range as a focus of economic life and as a creator of regional opinion.

Naturally, a regional centre which publishes a daily newspaper read over so extensive an area will contain several smaller urban fields, served by weekly newspapers only. There is, in fact, a ranking order (or hierarchy) of towns and associated urban fields. There is, at the head of the hierarchy, the metropolitan city of London, which may be called a first-order town because, in such spheres as government, entertainment, newspaper provision and medical specialist facilities, it serves the whole of Britain. On a slightly lower level of services, it shares certain functions such as larger and more specialized shops, University education facilities, etc., with second-order towns such as Manchester, Liverpool, Birmingham and Leeds. At this level, London is the centre only for what we justly call the Home Counties, and the other major cities named have an equal attraction for the people living within their respective fields. Within these again there are third-order towns, and within these are fourth-order towns which are little removed from large villages in size and significance to the areas surrounding them. Thus, at whatever stage in the hierarchy of towns, there is a direct relationship between the size and function of a town and of its urban field.

SECONDARY SCHOOLS AND COLLEGES OF FURTHER EDUCATION

Secondary Schools and Colleges of Further Education represent a centralized educational service for a fairly extensive area. The addresses of all pupils can be marked as dots on a map, and a line drawn to enclose the area from which the pupils are drawn: among educational administrators this is often called the 'catchment area' of the school or college. Its extent provides a measure of the influence of the town upon young people, who spend their most impressionable years within the ambit of one of the most important of the town's services (Fig. 51).

> Hatfield and Welwyn now have Grammar Schools for Girls, but no Boys' Grammar Schools.
> How does this affect catchment areas?
> Loreto College is the only Catholic Grammar School in the district.
> How is this shown by the size of its catchment area?

HOSPITALS AND EMERGENCY SERVICES

The service area of a hospital and its associated ambulance service indicates the range of a town's functions as a district medical centre (Fig. 52). The concept of an urban hierarchy may be observable here, for, although most sick persons are taken to the general hospital nearest their homes, certain cases may have to be taken longer distances to a larger regional hospital because this alone has such specialist equipment as kidney machines, or iron lungs, and the doctors specializing in the diagnosis and cure of certain rare and complicated illnesses.

The police and fire services also lay down the boundaries of the areas within which they undertake to cope with emergencies when summoned by a 999 telephone call (Fig. 52).

> Do you consider that the hospitals in the St. Albans area are conveniently placed to serve the population? There are important new housing estates to the north east and south of St. Albans.
> How does this affect the pattern of emergency services?

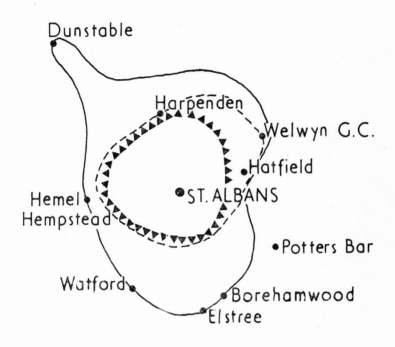

CATCHMENT AREAS OF ST. ALBANS SECONDARY SCHOOLS

Dunstable

Harpenden

Welwyn G.C.

Hatfield

ST. ALBANS

Hemel Hempstead

Potters Bar

Watford

Borehamwood

Elstree

—— Loreto College
--- St. Albans Boys' Grammar School
▲▲▲ St. Albans Girls' Grammar School

0   5   10
MILES

Fig. 51

EMERGENCY SERVICES OPERATING FROM ST. ALBANS

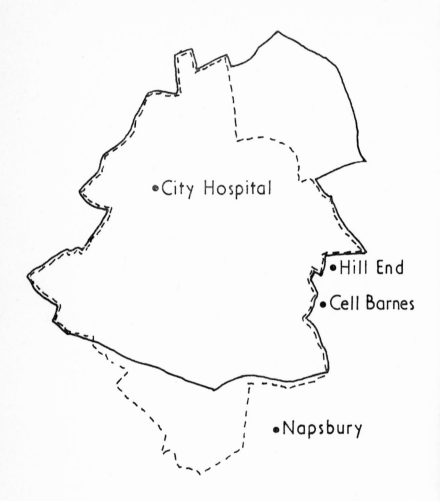

• City Hospital

• Hill End

• Cell Barnes

• Napsbury

• Hospitals
  Boundaries of Police area —
               Fire and Ambulance area----

⊢ 1 mile ⊣

Fig. 52

Do you feel that the boundaries of all service areas should be identical?

THE TOWN AS A CENTRE OF EMPLOYMENT

Some firms willingly provide information about the extent of the area within which they recruit employees. This can be the basis of another map (Fig. 53). If the information from a number of firms can be plotted on the same base-map, it may be seen that some firms draw their labour from a much more extensive area than others. If one town is very near another offering similar types of employment, there may well be competition for labour, resulting in expansions or contractions in the catchment areas of the rural employers.

Fig. 53 shows the labour catchment areas of a variety of factories in St. Albans. Ballito makes stockings, the Danish Bacon Company is mainly engaged in the distributive trade, Heath and Heather deals in seeds for gardens, Rodex manufacture ladies' coats and De la Rue is a printing firm.

Most firms rely on local transport to bring in employees, but one runs a private bus to Dunstable.

Which is this firm likely to be, from the evidence of Fig. 49?

Is there any correlation between this map and the one showing week-day bus transport to St. Albans (Fig. 47)?

THE JOURNEY TO WORK

The map of factory-employment in a town has close links with one showing the time it takes to reach the town from outlying places by public transport. Journey-time to work is best represented by isochrones, as has already been mentioned. Isochrones have been drawn on Fig. 49, with the assistance of bus timetables supplemented by personal experiences, to link all places which lie at $\frac{1}{4}$, $\frac{1}{2}$, $\frac{3}{4}$, 1 hr., $1\frac{1}{4}$ and $1\frac{1}{2}$ hours bus journey time from St. Albans.

What is the average travelling time for workers employed in the five St. Albans factories shown in Fig. 53?

What appears to be the maximum time which em-

LABOUR CATCHMENT AREAS OF SOME
ST. ALBANS FACTORIES

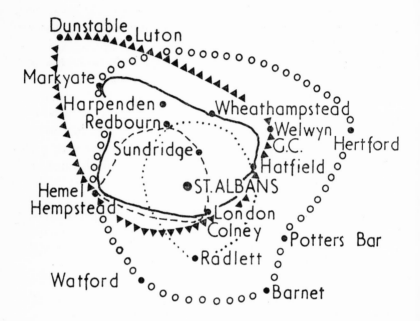

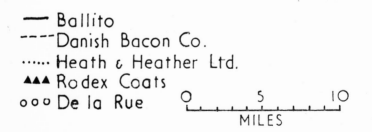

— Ballito
---- Danish Bacon Co.
..... Heath & Heather Ltd.
▲▲▲ Rodex Coats
○○○ De la Rue

0   5   10
MILES

Fig. 53

ployees are willing to travel in order to work in St. Albans?

What is one reason why so large a proportion of the workers in St. Albans' factories come from the north-west of the town?

Why does employment in St. Albans sharply fall off past Barnet and Potters Bar?

THE TOWN AS A COLLECTING AND DISTRIBUTING CENTRE

Towns are markets through which local products are channelled on their way to the outside world. They are also consuming centres for many of the products of their environs, notably fresh milk and vegetables. It is often possible, if representative organizations are prepared to make available the information which they possess, to make precise maps to illustrate the collecting function of a town. For example, an agricultural auctioneer may supply information regarding the farms from which he regularly received livestock for his sales; this will give an indication of the market-area. It may be possible also, to map the milk collection areas relating to particular consuming centres.

THE DELIVERY AREAS OF SHOPS

It is as centres for retail distribution, and as shopping centres, however, that the residents of the district surrounding a town have the most frequent and intimate association with the town. A recent survey among the villagers of Hampshire showed that four-fifths of them went out of their village for some shopping, two-fifths of them once a week and nearly a fifth more frequently. Two-thirds of the villagers' journeys were to a nearby town up to nine miles away, 16 per cent were to regional centres and one per cent to London.

It is rarely possible to obtain a list of customers with accounts at a particular shop in town, but much the same result is obtained by mapping the areas within which retail shops undertake regular van-deliveries of goods which customers have ordered by telephone or selected in a visit to the shop (Fig. 54).

131

DELIVERY AREAS OF SOME SHOPS IN ST. ALBANS

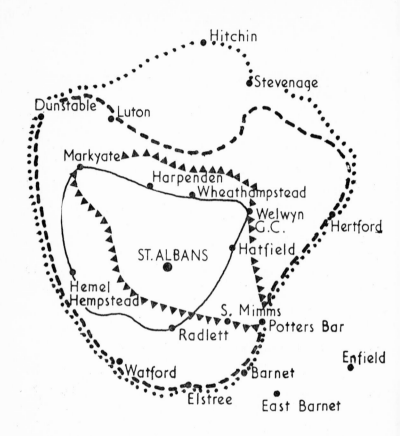

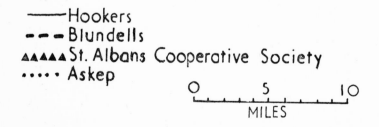

——— Hookers
– – – Blundells
▲▲▲▲▲ St. Albans Cooperative Society
••••• Askep

0   5   10
MILES

Fig. 54

Blundells and the St. Albans Co-operative Society are departmental stores, with branches at Watford and Luton.

What effect does this have upon the delivery areas of these firms?

Hookers is a firm which supplies glass, and specializes in stained glass. Askeys deals in secondhand furniture. Why is their field of delivery much more extensive?

MILK DELIVERY

Another pattern of delivery is that of fresh milk (Fig. 55). Fresh milk cannot travel very far, or else it cannot be delivered early enough in the morning for customers to use it. The pattern of delivery may be distorted somewhat by the agreements which milkmen are encouraged to make in order to cut down the effort and cost of ensuring that every household may find bottles of milk on the doorstep every morning. Nevertheless, milk delivery reveals one aspect of the town's function as a distributive centre.

THE MARGINS OF URBAN FIELDS

The relationships between town and surrounding area are essentially fluid, and hence the margins of an urban field are not accurately represented by a firm, constant line. Nor does the urban field extend with even intensity to a certain limit and then suddenly stop short; in fact, it grades off imperceptibly until there comes an arbitrary point through which it is decided to draw the limiting line. Nor is the margin of an urban field a single line, but there are as many different versions of the area served by an urban centre as there are particular services or functions which the town performs. Nevertheless, versions of the extent of the field display so many similarities that the advantages of the method far outweigh its limitations.

The task of delimiting urban fields has important practical applications. The administrative boundaries of our towns frequently need revision, as new housing estates are added, in order that the administrative area may correspond with the community area. However carefully the boundaries of a town may have at one time been drawn to take account of geographical

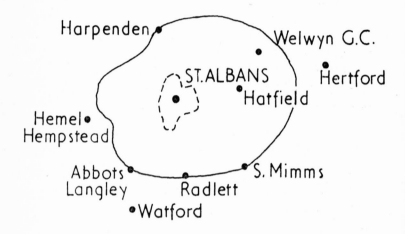

— St. Albans Co-operative Society
---- Express Dairy

0   5   10
MILES

Fig. 55

facts and real social ties, they are soon outdated, and need redrawing.

ARE COUNTY BOUNDARIES OBSOLETE?

Boundaries of urban fields are no respecters of county boundaries. So often do the spheres of influence cross with county boundaries which in many places were drawn almost a thousand years ago, that many people advocate the abolition of counties and the redrawing of the administrative map of England and Wales on the basis of an assumption that there is now no part of these counties which does not fall within the sphere of influence of one town or another.

STATISTICS OF TOWNS

For every town, statistics are available which answer the
questions, 'How much?' and 'How many?' We should aim at
collecting such statistics, and representing as many of them as
possible in map form, so that they answer the question 'Where?'
as well.

POPULATION STATISTICS AND
THEIR REPRESENTATION

Census Reports are to be found in the larger Public Libraries,
and these give a wealth of information about the number of
people who live in various areas. Every ten years since 1801, a
national Census has been taken by means of questionnaires completed by householders and returned to a Government official
known as the Registrar-General. He publishes a summary of the
information in bulky volumes of statistical tables. These show,
not only the number of people living in each ward of a town on
Census night, but also the number of men and women, the
numbers engaged in various occupations, as well as details of
the housing arrangements such as the number of rooms, the
availability of piped water and baths, etc.

Wards of towns tend to be so large and varied that statistics
relating to wards as a whole are of limited value. For more precise information on the location of population the best source is
the annual Register of Electors which provides for each polling
district the names and addresses of all adults entitled to vote at
elections. Copies of the Register can be obtained for a small fee
from the Electoral Registration Officer, who is usually the Town
Clerk, or Clerk to the Urban District Council, or they can be
consulted in any of the larger Post Offices.

We make a dot distribution map of a group of streets by placing a dot for, say, every five persons, upon each house as shown
on a large scale Ordnance Survey map, say on a scale of 25 to 50

136

inches to a mile (Fig. 56). The resultant map shows tremendous variations in density of population. A second map may be drawn to emphasize this fact by substituting for the dots a series of lines separating the areas of highest density from those of medium density, and these in turn from areas of low density. The method is shown in Figs. 56 and 57. Rule a grid of small squares over the face of the map, count the number of dots falling within each square and write the number clearly within the square. Choose a number which represents a really high density, say fifty per half inch square, i.e. 1200 sq. yards on the ground, and draw a line enclosing all the squares which have more than this number. Then take a number which represents a low density, such as 25 per square, and draw a second line to envelop these. The spaces between the two lines will therefore be the areas of medium density. The lines should be smoothly flowing ones, rather than lines clinging to the edges of squares and so making many right-angled bends. They must therefore cross squares; a glance at the original dot-distribution map will show where within each square the density changes, and act as a guide for the placing of the lines. Such lines, enclosing areas of roughly equal density, are known as isopleths (Fig. 58).

What is the maximum number of persons in a single house shown in Fig. 56? (Remember that each dot represents five persons.)

What is the minimum number of persons in a house of somewhat similar size?

Are there any non-residential areas? How do the shapes and sizes of non-residential buildings differ from the residential ones?

Do you consider the area to be in general over-crowded?

Is there adequate play space for children in gardens, etc.?

Are there any streets which could be profitably closed to traffic and used as 'play streets'?

Did you find that, even though you followed the method of drawing isopleths set out in the text, you obtained a slightly different result? It would not be at all surprising if this were so.

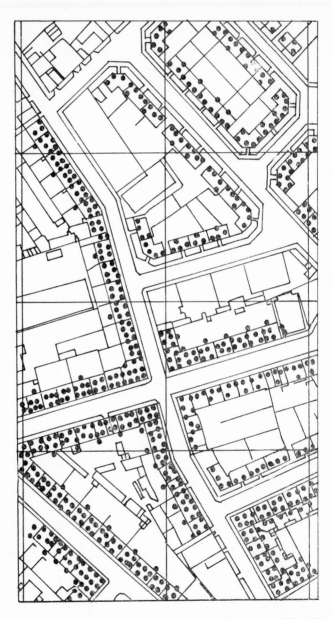

Scale:
1:2,500

Fig. 56

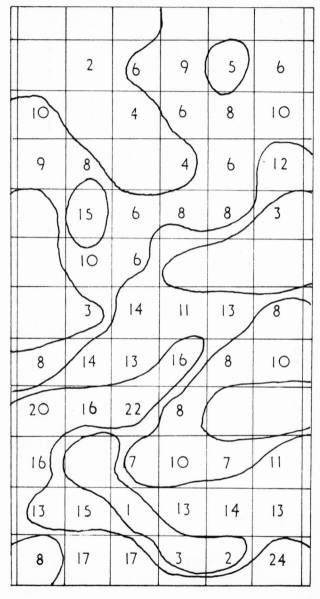

Fig. 57

POPULATION ISOPLETH MAP

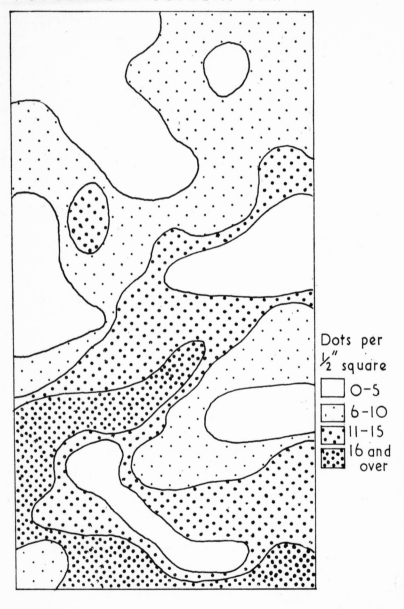

Dots per ½" square

☐ 0-5

6-10

11-15

16 and over

Fig. 58

OCCUPATIONAL STATISTICS

The Census attempts to give not only the number of people, but also the kinds of work they do. The chief difficulty in providing this information is to fit into a list of occupations of manageable length the people whose jobs are out of the ordinary. Thus in potteries we may find 'saggers bottom knockers', and in printing works we may find 'banknote finishers' and in many trades we find 'twisters'.

Occupational statistics have the disadvantage that they relate to the kind of work a person does, irrespective of the industry which employs him, and therefore the twenty-seven main categories contain such groups as 'clerks and typists', 'persons engaged in transport' and 'workers in unskilled occupations' irrespective of the particular industry to which they belong.

INDUSTRIAL STATISTICS

A second set of figures, the *Industry Tables*, appears in Census Reports, in which every worker appears again but this time classified by the industry which employs him, irrespective of what job he does, whether as managing director of a chocolate factory or the girl who puts the ribbon round the completed boxes of chocolates.

For some industries, additional local information may be obtained from a Year Book published by either some particular industry or by the town authorities themselves. Thus the *Colliery Year Book and Coal Trades Directory* lists the numbers of men employed above and below ground, and the annual production at each colliery in Britain. In addition, most of the nationalized industries and organizations publish an Annual Report or similarly titled volume containing varying amounts of statistics.

PLACE OF WORK AND PLACE OF RESIDENCE

Many people live in one place and work in another, travelling daily to their work in a different place from the place where they reside. Such people are often styled commuters.

The Census volumes are a source from which statistics may be gathered to show the numbers travelling to work, both into a place and away from a place. Figs. 59 and 60 show these numbers for the town of St. Albans in Hertfordshire.

Which appears to be the larger – the total number of people leaving St. Albans to work or the number of people coming into St. Albans to work?

Which town is by far the largest receiver of persons leaving St. Albans each day?

This is because it has aircraft factories and a large Technical school, as well as a new shopping centre and caters for tourists who come to visit the mansion of Hatfield House.

Which town receives the second largest number of daily workers with homes in St. Albans?

This is because it has a large variety of industrial and business concerns, often with headquarters in London.

Is the flow mainly towards London or away from it into the Hertfordshire countryside?

Why should this be so?

Why do you think comparatively few people go to Hertford, which has the County administrative offices?

Is daily movement into St. Albans mainly from the London side or from the N. Hertfordshire side?

How do you account for the contrast between the pattern of inflow and the pattern of outflow in this respect?

Harpenden is very much a residential town, with few industrial opportunities. The St. Albans Girls' Grammar School is also on the Harpenden side of the town.

How are these facts reflected in the flow pattern?

Which town on the west side of St. Albans sends less workers to St. Albans than its neighbours?

Is this connected with the fact that it has a new industrial estate, specializing in photographic products?

Is it correct to call St. Albans a mere dormitory town and supplier of labour to London? Or has it an independent life of its own?

EMIGRATION FROM AND IMMIGRATION TO A TOWN

A very interesting Census volume gives for each town, urban or rural district, the number of people who have ceased to live there, or have made it their home, during the ten years since the last census, i.e. during the decade 1951–61. What is more, the Census of Migration tables show the chief areas to and from which the movements took place over the ten years.

Fig. 61 (p. 146) shows the details of movements to and from St. Albans between 1951 and 1961.

> Who are the most mobile, men or women?
> How can you account for this?
> Is it related to marriage to men who are settled in jobs?
> Do women, on leaving St. Albans, tend on the whole to move a shorter distance or a longer distance to their new homes than the men do?
> Is St. Albans gaining or losing on the whole, from these inward and outward movements?
> Is the loss mainly of men or of women?
> Ravenstein, a famous writer on population movements, stated in 1886 that people who move tend to move a short distance rather than a long one.
> Is this true of St. Albans?
> Is St. Albans acquiring a large overseas-born element in its population or not?
> Would you be able to meet many recent emigrants from St. Albans in overseas countries or not?
> Can you suggest reasons for the St. Albans people's attitude to emigration?

THE GEOMETRY OF A TOWN

The key to understanding the success or failure of a town's layout to satisfy the needs of its inhabitants often lies in the geometrical features of the town-unit. In the first place, it is important if a town is to work well that it should be compact, and should have a centre which is comfortably accessible from all parts. This will depend upon the shape and area of the town, and the features of its boundary. In the second place, the

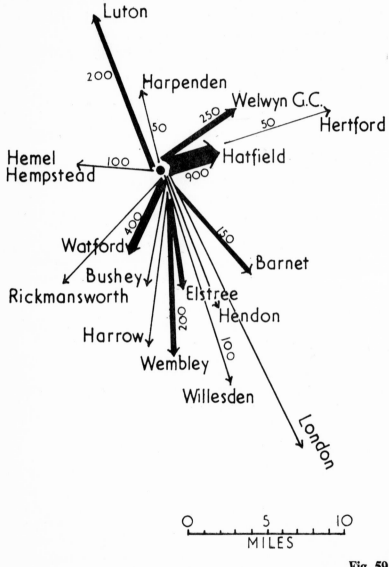

Fig. 59

THE JOURNEY TO WORK IN ST. ALBANS

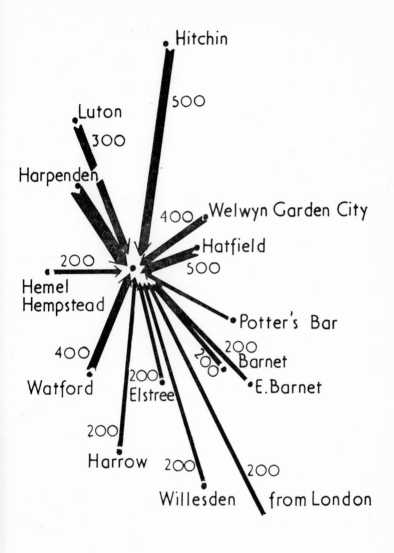

Hitchin
500

Luton
300

Harpenden

400 · Welwyn Garden City

· Hatfield
500

200
Hemel
Hempstead

· Potter's Bar

200
200 Barnet
200
· E. Barnet

400

200
Elstree

Watford

200

Harrow 200

200

Willesden from London

0   5   10
MILES

Fig. 60

145

POPULATION MOVEMENTS TO AND FROM
ST. ALBANS
1951–61

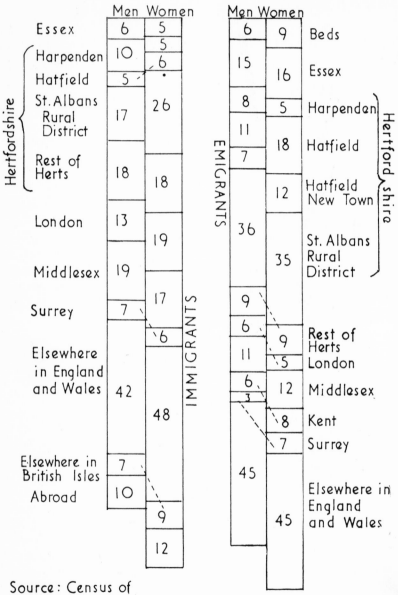

Source: Census of
Migration Tables No.7

Fig. 61

constituent units of the town, such as the suburban wards which are the units of administration, and the areas served to shopping centres which are the units of commerce, should be well spaced and of a size which enable them to work well.

THE BASIC SHAPE OF A TOWN

The extent to which a town or city is conveniently shaped and its hub suitably placed, may be studied by three methods.

Trace the outer edge of a map of the built up area on squared paper, as has been done for Birmingham in Fig. 62. Fortunately, for Birmingham this line is almost identical with the administrative boundary. The area is then calculated by counting the number of squares, making allowance for the incomplete ones, and multiplying by the area of one square. Draw and measure the longest and the shortest axes, i.e. the longest and the shortest lines which it is possible to draw between points on the perimeter. Measure their lengths and note their point of intersection in relationship to the present city centre. In the ideally shaped city, the two axes should be of similar length and should intersect at the existing centre of the city.

How far does the shape of Birmingham measure up to the ideal?

Calculate the ratio between the length of Birmingham's perimeter and its area, with the aid of the figure.

Repeat the procedure for other towns, particularly any in Britain (such as Glasgow) or abroad which have roughly the same number of people as Birmingham. Compare the suitability of their shapes for maximizing convenience of administration and of access to and from the centre.

Draw the smallest possible circle which will enclose a tracing of the shape of the entire town, searching by experiment for the appropriate centre and radius which will ensure this aim. Next draw the largest circle which will entirely fit within the town's boundaries, again searching by experiment for the most convenient centre and radius for this circle. Note also the existing centre of the town, as has been done for Birmingham in Fig. 63.

TO CALCULATE BIRMINGHAM'S AREA PERIMETER AND LENGTH OF LONGEST AXIS

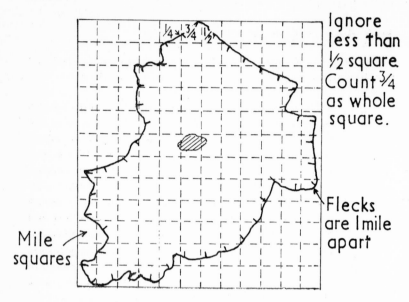

¼→ ¾ 1½

Ignore less than ½ square. Count ¾ as whole square.

Flecks are 1 mile apart

Mile squares

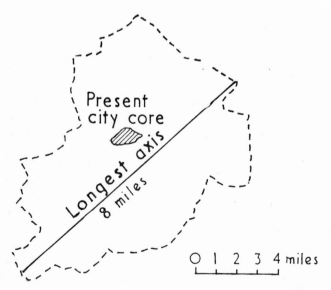

Present city core

Longest axis 8 miles

O 1 2 3 4 miles

Fig. 62

Join the three possible centres for Birmingham so far obtained, to make a triangle.

Explore the advantages and disadvantages of resiting the centre, not only in terms of the townspeople themselves but also from the point of view of the people in the surrounding district which is largely dependent upon the city for employment and services.

Draw within a tracing of the town's boundaries a polygon with the smallest number of sides which will best fill the enclosed shape. Subdivide this polygon into triangles with a common apex towards the centre, finding its position by experiment. This has been done for Birmingham in Fig 64.

Does the apex of the triangle correspond with the present hub of the city?

If not, what would be gained by resiting the city centre near the place which has been arrived at by this geometrical experiment?

How does the centre arrived at by this method compare with the two other centres arrived at by the method of drawing an inscribed circle and a circumscribed circle (Fig. 63)?

It will be convenient if the city's wards roughly occupy the various triangular wedges shown on the diagram.

Do any of these have such a triangular form?

In what cases does an inner ward added to an outer ward assume this triangular form?

Would the problems which arise in administering the present wards be greater if the wards were of much more irregular shape?

Should any wards be enlarged or reduced to make them more convenient in shape?

THE GEOMETRY OF A CITY'S SHAPE: BIRMINGHAM

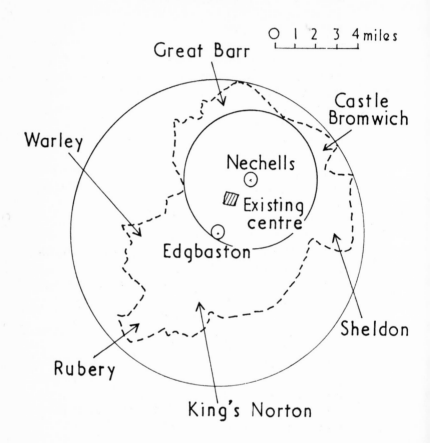

The largest circle fitting within Birmingham's boundary, and the smallest circle enclosing it, are shown.

Fig. 63

BIRMINGHAM AS A POLYGON

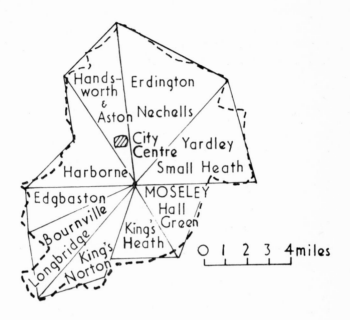

Note that the apex of constituent triangles, at Moseley, is far from the city centre but close to the old industrial core.

Many leading suburbs tend to correspond with the triangular wedges.

Fig. 64

ACKNOWLEDGEMENTS

The author expresses deep gratitude to those many former pupils whose fieldwork forms the basis of many of the examples used in the book, and in particular to Janette Savage, B.A., and Opal Lankester. Mr. Edgar Jackson kindly provided the material for figs. 29 and 30. Mrs. Marguerite Urwin gave great help with the illustrations. The frontispiece photograph is by A. F. Kersting and the cover photograph by Aerofilm Ltd.

INDEX